Best Easy Day Hikes
Colorado Springs

D0880644

Help Us Keep This Guide Up to Date

Every effort has been made by the authors and editors to make this guide as accurate and useful as possible. However, many things can change after a guide is published—trails are rerouted, regulations change, facilities come under new management, and so on.

We would appreciate hearing from you concerning your experiences with this guide and how you feel it could be improved and kept up to date. While we may not be able to respond to all comments and suggestions, we'll take them to heart and we'll also make certain to share them with the authors. Please send your comments and suggestions to the following address:

FalconGuides
Reader Response/Editorial Department
246 Goose Lane
Guilford, CT 06437

Or you may e-mail us at:

editorial@Falcon.com

Thanks for your input, and happy trails!

Best Easy Day Hikes Series

Best Easy Day Hikes
Colorado Springs

Third Edition

Stewart M. Green and
Tracy Salcedo

FALCONGUIDES

GUILFORD, CONNECTICUT

FALCONGUIDES®

An imprint of The Rowman & Littlefield Publishing Group, Inc., 4501 Forbes Blvd., Ste. 200, Lanham, MD 20706
Falcon and FalconGuides are registered trademarks and Make Adventure Your Story is a trademark of Rowman & Littlefield.

Distributed by NATIONAL BOOK NETWORK

British Library Cataloguing-in-Publication Information available

The Library of Congress has catalogued a previous edition as follows:

Names: Green, Stewart M., author
Title: Best easy day hikes Colorado Springs/Stewart M. Green and Tracy Salcedo.
Description: Guilford, Connecticut : FalconGuides, 2011.
Identifiers: LCCN 2011016365 | ISBN 9780762763573 (pbk. : alk. paper)
Subjects: LCSH: Hiking—Colorado—Colorado Springs Region—Guidebooks.
Trails—Colorado—Colorado Springs Region—Guidebooks.
Colorado Springs Region (Colo.)—Guidebooks.
Classification: LCC GV199.42.C62 C6436 2011 | DDC 917.88/560434—dc22 LC record available at https://lccn.loc.gov/2011016365

ISBN 978-1-4930-3014-9 (paperback)
ISBN 978-1-4930-3015-6 (e-book)

∞™ The paper used in this publication meets the minimum requirements of American National Standard for Information Sciences—Permanence of Paper for Printed Library Materials, ANSI/NISO Z39.48-1992.

Printed in the United States of America

Contents

The Hikes

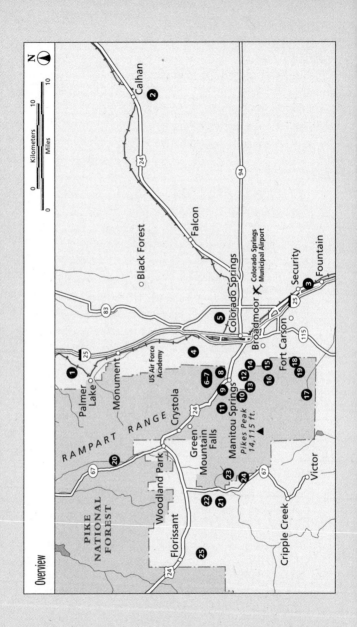

Overview

Introduction

Colorado Springs is famed for its many recreational opportunities, beginning in the nineteenth century when visitors came for its mild climate and glorious natural wonders. The area has it all—long vistas of mountains, prairie, and sky; stunning attractions like Pikes Peak and the Garden of the Gods; and over 1,000 miles of trails.

The greater Colorado Springs area offers excellent trails that thread through canyons, climb mountains, and traverse forests and grasslands. *Best Easy Day Hikes Colorado Springs* describes the best hikes and trails for the casual hiker within 35 miles of the city.

If you are on a tight schedule or want to do a short hike in a scenic area, the hikes in this book allow you to quickly select a day hike suited to your abilities and time constraints. Many of the hikes are between 1 and 3 miles long. Also included are nature walks for families and barrier-free trails that are wheelchair accessible. All the trailheads are easily reached by vehicle and have parking lots; some have facilities including water and restrooms. The hikes are rated by difficulty, being either easy or moderate. Check the Trail Finder to help you decide which hike is best for your party.

One of the best ways to enjoy, understand, and appreciate Colorado is by hiking its diverse terrain. Footpaths take you away from highways and roads and into ancient landscapes preserved in the rarified air, past ponds ringed with windswept grass, under shining mountains, and to the summits of high peaks with views that go on forever. Every hiker interested in Colorado Springs' varied ecosystems, which range from semi desert and prairie to wet woodlands and the barren land above the trees, can learn much by hiking the region's many trails.

Best Easy Day Hikes Colorado Springs is about walking for pleasure—about the joy of putting on boots, shouldering a pack, and setting off into the world. Pick an easy trail and follow your feet. You'll find you can go just about anywhere.

Leave No Trace

Colorado Springs is an outdoors city. The US Olympic Committee is headquartered in Colorado Springs. World-class runners and mountain bikers train on Colorado Springs' trails. One of the area's big sporting events is the Pikes Peak Marathon—26 miles and 8,000 vertical feet up and down America's most famous mountain. In 2009 *Outside* magazine rated Colorado Springs #1 as the "Best Place to Live," while *Men's Fitness* magazine ranked it #2 as the "Fittest City in America," and *Women's Health* magazine ranked it #10 as the "Best Place to Be a Woman." Colorado Springs is simply a great place to get outside and enjoy wild nature.

With all the hikers in the Colorado Springs region, it's important to practice a Leave No Trace philosophy so that the area's natural resources and trails are protected from over-use and to maintain a positive experience for all visitors. Use the following Leave No Trace suggestions to make your own as well as everyone else's visit enjoyable and to protect our spectacular natural world.

Leave No Trace is about responsible outdoor ethics, including staying on the trail, not cutting switchbacks, packing out litter, keeping your dog leashed and picking up its waste, disposing properly of human waste, and leaving the environment as pristine as possible. Mountain and prairie ecosystems and environments are fragile and sensitive to human use. The marks of man, including social trails and damage from all-terrain vehicles and motorcycles, linger for years on this landscape.

Every hiker should adopt the Leave No Trace ethic to minimize his or her impact on this beautiful land. It's our responsibility to pay attention to our impact so that we can ensure that these trails will remain as wild refuges from the urban environment.

Always stay on the trail. Cutting switchbacks or traveling cross-country causes erosion and destroys plants. Always follow the route whenever possible. Steep slopes are susceptible to erosion caused by off-trail hiking.

Pack it in—pack it out. Everything you carry and use, including food wrappers, orange peels, cigarette butts, plastic bottles, and energy bar wrappers, needs to come out with you. Carry a plastic bag for picking up trash along the trail. Also, pick up your dog's waste and pack it out in a plastic bag. Too many dog owners leave their pet's feces on the trail.

Respect public and private property, livestock fences, and mining claims. Federal laws protect all archaeological and historic antiquities, including Native American artifacts, projectile points, ruins, petroglyphs, petrified wood, and historic sites. Don't carve your name on a rock surface or on a tree.

Properly dispose of human waste by digging a hole 4 to 6 inches deep and at least 300 feet from water sources and dry washes. Do not burn or bury toilet paper. Instead, pack it out in a plastic baggie. The best thing to do is to use the public restrooms found at many trailheads.

Take only photographs and memories. We can avoid leaving evidence of our passage across this delicate mountain environment. With care and sensitivity, we can all do our part to keep the Colorado Springs region beautiful, clean, and pristine. Leave natural features such as flowers or rocks where you found them. Enjoy their beauty, but leave them for the next hiker. If everyone took one item, it wouldn't be long before nothing was left for others to enjoy.

For more information visit LNT.org.

Be Prepared

Hiking, although immensely rewarding, also comes with hazards and inherent risks, especially for those who come unprepared. Respect the mountain environment; be prepared and you'll be safe.

You must assume responsibility for your own actions and for your safety. Be aware of your surroundings and of potential dangers, including drop-offs, cliffs, and loose rock; the weather; and the physical condition of both your party and yourself. Never be afraid to turn around if conditions aren't right. Pay attention to those bad feelings—they could keep you alive.

Here are a few suggestions to be prepared for emergency situations on your hike:

- Bring extra clothes and a raincoat, especially in the mountains. The weather can change in an instant. Heavy thunderstorms regularly occur on summer afternoons, and cold, wet clothing can lead to hypothermia.
- Colorado's Front Range has more lightning strikes than almost anywhere else in the United States. Pay attention to the weather, and get off high places before a storm arrives. If you can hear thunder, it's probably not safe to be outdoors.

- The air is thin and the sun is bright in the mountains. Summer temperatures can be hot. Wear a hat and use sunscreen to avoid sunburn.
- Carry plenty of water and sports drinks to replace electrolytes lost through sweating. Don't drink any water from streams unless you first treat and purify it.
- If you're coming from a lower elevation, watch for symptoms of altitude sickness, including headache, nausea, and loss of appetite. The best cure is to lose elevation.
- Allow enough time for your hike. If you start in late afternoon, bring a headlamp or flashlight so that you can see the trail in the dark.
- Bring plenty of high-energy snacks for the trail and treats for the youngsters.
- Wear comfortable hiking shoes and good socks. Your feet will thank you. To avoid blisters, break in your shoes before wearing them in the backcountry.
- Enjoy the wildlife you see along the trail, but keep your distance and treat the animals with respect. Those cute little animals can bite and spread diseases like rabies. Watchful mothers, including deer and black bears, are protective of their babies. Rattlesnakes are found on low-elevation trails, so watch where you place your hands and feet. Don't feed wildlife to avoid disrupting their natural eating habits.
- Carry a day pack to tote all your trail needs, including rain gear, food, water, a first-aid kit, a flashlight, matches, and extra clothes. A whistle, GPS unit, topo map, binoculars, camera, pocketknife, and FalconGuide identification books for plants and animals are all handy additions. And don't forget your copy of *Best Easy Day Hikes Colorado Springs*!

Trail Finder

Best Hikes for Great Views

    4. Ute Valley Park Loop
    6. Perkins Central Garden Trail
  10. Red Mountain Trail
  12. Red Rock Canyon Trail
  17. Gray Back Peak Trail
  22. Grouse Mountain Overlook Trail

Best Hikes for Waterfalls

  16. Silver Cascade Falls Trail
  24. Horsethief Park Trail

Best Hikes with Children

    3. Fountain Creek Nature Trail
    6. Perkins Central Garden Trail
    9. Siamese Twins Trail
  18. Coyote Run Trail
  20. Manitou Lake Trail
  25. Petrified Forest Loop and Ponderosa Loop Trails

Best Hikes for Wildlife

    3. Fountain Creek Nature Trail
  21. Outlook Ridge and Lost Pond Loop
  25. Petrified Forest Loop and Ponderosa Loop Trails

Best Hikes for Photographers

    2. Paint Mines Trail
    6. Perkins Central Garden Trail
    7. Susan G. Bretag Trail and Palmer Trail Loop
  13. Contemplative Trail to Sand Canyon Trail Loop
  23. The Crags Trail

Best Summit Hikes

1. Spruce Mountain Trail
10. Red Mountain Trail
15. Mount Cutler Trail
17. Gray Back Peak Trail
22. Grouse Mountain Overlook Trail

Best Hikes for Solitude

1. Spruce Mountain Trail
17. Gray Back Peak Trail
19. Blackmer Loop Trail

Map Legend

	Interstate Highway
	US Highway
	State Highway
	Local Road
	Unpaved Road
	Featured Trail
	Trail
	Railroad
	River/Creek
	Intermittent Stream
	Local/State Park
	National Forest
	Marsh/Swamp
	Bridge
	Campground
	Gate
	Mountain/Peak
	Parking
	Picnic Area
	Point of Interest/Structure
	Restroom
	Tower
	Town
	Trailhead
	Tunnel
	Viewpoint/Overlook
	Visitor/Information Center
	Waterfall

1 Spruce Mountain Trail

This wonderful hike climbs to the eastern end of Spruce Mountain's long summit and follows a loop trail through an open pine woodland to Windy Point at the mountain's west end.

Distance: 5.3-mile double loop
Hiking time: 3 to 4 hours
Difficulty: Moderate; 505-foot elevation gain
Trail surface: Single- and doubletrack dirt path
Best season: Year-round; icy in winter
Other trail users: Mountain bikers, runners, equestrians
Canine compatibility: Leashed dogs permitted
Fees and permits: No fees or permits required

Schedule: Open Space open from one hour before sunrise to one hour after sunset
Maps: USGS Larkspur; trail map available at Douglas County Open Space website
Trail contacts: Douglas County Division of Open Space and Natural Resources, 100 Third St., Castle Rock, CO 80104; (303) 660-7495; www.douglas .co.us/government/departments /open-space/

Finding the trailhead: From Colorado Springs drive north on I-25 past Monument. At the top of Monument Hill, take exit 163 and turn left (west) onto County Line Road, which you follow to the north side of Palmer Lake. After crossing railroad tracks, the road dead-ends against Spruce Mountain Road/Douglas CR 53. Turn right (north) and drive 3.5 miles; turn left into the marked Spruce Mountain Open Space parking lot. The trailhead is at the west end of the parking lot. GPS: 39.167896, –104.874792

The Hike

The Spruce Mountain Trail is a wonderful hike north of Palmer Lake and east of the Rampart Range, a low mountain range that runs from Ute Pass to the South Platte River. The trail climbs to the eastern end of Spruce Mountain and then makes a long loop, following first the mountain's southern rim to its rocky 7,605-foot summit before returning along its northern rim.

Expect easy hiking on a good single- and doubletrack trail with gradual grades, open ponderosa pine and scrub oak woodlands, and spacious views from Pikes Peak to Longs Peak. The trail and mountain are on Spruce Mountain Open Space land, which was purchased by Douglas County between 2000 and 2009 to protect it from development as a resort with a hotel on the mountain, a golf course, and luxury homes.

Begin from the trailhead at the parking area on the west side of Spruce Mountain Road, north of Palmer Lake. The only amenities are a bear-proof trash container and a portable toilet. Remember to pack out your trash, keep your dog leashed, pick up its waste, and stay on the trails—no shortcutting! Keep an eye out for mountain bikers and equestrians on this multiuse trail.

Pass through a gate and walk 350 feet to a trail junction. Go straight on the Spruce Mountain Trail and pass through a dense scrub oak thicket. Continue west up the slowly rising trail across open meadows on the northern slope of Spruce Mountain. Eagle Mountain rises to the northwest, ringed by high sandstone cliffs like an ancient battlement. After 0.3 mile go left at a trail junction, signed "Mountain Top Loop," on Spruce Mountain Trail. Eagle Pass Trail goes straight.

The singletrack trail bends left and contours up the north flank of Spruce Mountain. The damp north-facing slope is covered in a mixed forest of scrub oak, ponderosa pine, fir, and spruce. After 0.3 mile of climbing, the trail reaches a junction on a slight knoll with Oak Shortcut Trail. Go right on the main trail.

The next 0.5 mile of trail is the toughest section of the hike. The trail switchbacks up the wooded east side of the mountain, passing beneath a jutting outcrop of Dawson arkose (a coarse sandstone) before crossing onto the cooler northern slope. After climbing 0.6 mile from the last junction (1.2 miles from the trailhead), you reach Greenland Overlook, a lofty viewpoint that looks out over the rolling grasslands of Greenland Open Space. More good views are southwest toward 14,115-foot Pikes Peak, which rises beyond Mount Herman.

The trail climbs and passes onto the north side of Spruce Mountain's long cliff-rimmed summit and reaches Paddock's Point, a rocky viewpoint that looks north toward 7,515-foot Eagle Mountain. Continue up the trail through dry pine woods to the Y junction for the 2.3-mile Mountain Top Loop, which follows the south rim out to Windy Point and then back along the north rim to this junction. Go left on the doubletrack trail. This junction is 1.6 miles from the trailhead.

Follow the wide trail for the next 0.8 mile along the airy south rim of Spruce Mountain. Some strategically placed benches and picnic tables make good snack stops. The trail dips across broad ravines, climbs gentle slopes, and passes lots of rock-rimmed overlooks. None of these overlooks are fenced, and all are dangerous, with vertical drops of 60 feet. Keep a close watch on small children. The cliff rim is soft and loose.

After hiking 2.8 miles from the trailhead, you reach Windy Point, the 7,605-foot high point of Spruce Mountain, on the far western edge of the summit plateau. This exposed overlook makes a good break. Look southwest to Palmer Lake, cradled in a broad valley; snowcapped Pikes Peak rises beyond. This overlook is dangerous. Keep away from the cliff edge.

The next trail segment runs 0.4 mile northeast from Windy Point to a junction with the service road. Go right on the doubletrack loop trail for the described hike. (*Option:* A left turn on the service road descends 0.5 mile to Eagle Pass Trail, which you follow east for 1.8 miles back to the trailhead.)

To complete the upper loop trail, hike 0.7 mile along the wooded north rim to the end of the loop at the Y junction. Go straight on the main trail. It is 1.4 miles from here to the trailhead. Retrace your steps back to Greenland Overlook and then down the switchbacks to Pine Junction. Instead of going left on Spruce Mountain Trail, turn right onto Oak Shortcut Trail. Descend this short steep trail for 0.2 mile to a junction with Spruce Meadows Trail. Go left (north) and follow the trail downhill for 0.2 mile to a junction with Spruce Mountain Trail. Go right and walk a few hundred feet to the trailhead and the end of a great hike.

Miles and Directions

- **0.0** Begin at the trailhead (GPS: 39.167896, -104.874792). After about 350 feet reach a junction with the Spruce Meadows Trail. Go straight on the Spruce Mountain Trail.
- **0.3** Reach a junction with the Eagle Pass Trail (GPS: 39.167804, -104.881156). Go left.

Spruce Mountain Trail

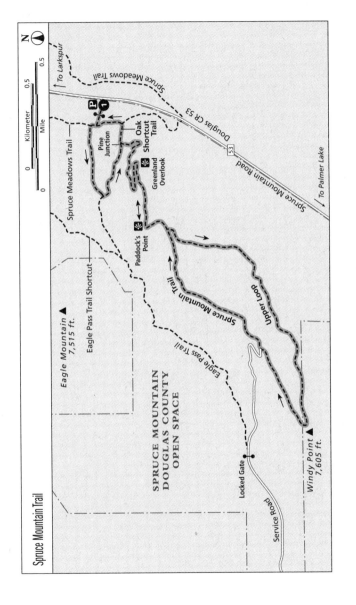

0.6 Go right at the junction with the Oak Shortcut Trail.

1.2 Arrive at Greenland Overlook.

1.6 Reach the junction with Mountain Top Loop Trail (GPS: 39.163626, −104.883723). Go left on the doubletrack trail.

2.8 Arrive at Windy Point (GPS: 39.155516, −104.898723). Go left 100 feet to the overlook and then backtrack to the loop trail.

3.2 Reach a junction with a service road. Go right on the trail.

3.9 Return to the start of the Mountain Top Loop Trail. Go straight.

4.9 At Pine Junction go right onto Oak Shortcut Trail.

5.0 Reach a junction with Spruce Meadows Trail. Go left.

5.2 Reach a junction with Spruce Mountain Trail. Go right 350 feet to the parking lot.

5.3 Arrive back at the trailhead and parking lot.

2 Paint Mines Trail

This loop hike in Paint Mines Interpretive Park traverses prairie grasslands to an eroded badlands of colorful sandstone used by ancient Native Americans for paint and pottery.

Distance: 3.7-mile double loop
Hiking time: 1.5 to 3 hours
Difficulty: Easy; 205-foot elevation gain
Trail surface: Single- and doubletrack dirt path
Best season: Year-round; hot in summer
Other trail users: Hikers only
Canine compatibility: No dogs allowed

Fees and permits: No fees or permits required
Maps: USGS Calhan; park map available at website
Trail contacts: El Paso County Parks and Leisure Services, 2002 Creek Crossing, Colorado Springs, CO 80905; (719) 520-PLAY (7529); http://adm.elpasoco .com/CommunityServices/Park Operations/Pages/default.aspx parks.com

Finding the trailhead: Drive east from Colorado Springs on US 24 for about 25 miles to Calhan. On the east side of Calhan, turn right (south) onto Yoder Street, which becomes Calhan Highway. Drive south on the road for 0.5 mile to Paint Mine Road. Turn left (east) on Paint Mine Road and drive to a large parking area and trailhead on the left. There's a restroom at the parking area. Another parking lot is 0.6 mile farther along the road on the south side of the park. GPS: 39.020863, -104.268546

The Hike

The Paint Mines Trail explores the high prairie and an unusual badlands south of Calhan in eastern El Paso County.

The single- and doubletrack trail has easy grades, interpretive signs, and lots of history. It can be hot in summer, and there is no shade. Wear a hat and bring plenty of water.

The Paint Mines, eroded badlands south of Calhan and US 24, are a wonderful off-the-beaten-track place. Eroded into a bluff, the Paint Mines area is filled with narrow canyons, rounded alabaster-white boulders, and rainbow-dyed hoodoos. The colorful mines, however, are only one part of the 753-acre Paint Mines Interpretive Park, which spreads across a grassy valley and protects a swath of short-grass prairie.

The Paint Mines form a miniature painted desert that was frequented by Native Americans for 10,000 years. They mined colored clay for ceramics and for pigments to paint pottery and used petrified wood for projectile points. In the late 1800s settlers used the clay to make bricks. The Paint Mines are listed on the National Register of Historic Places for their prehistoric significance.

Begin the hike at the trailhead on the east side of the parking lot off Paint Mine Road. There is a restroom at the parking area but no water. The hike goes clockwise, following two loop trails across the prairie before finishing at the Paint Mines area.

Begin by hiking east 0.1 mile to a three-way intersection. Go straight (east). (*Option:* A right turn will take you 0.7 mile south to the Paint Mines if you want to go there first.)

The first trail segment makes a 1.1-mile loop across prairie and up a dry drainage. Hike northeast for 0.4 mile on the wide trail to an interpretive sign that explains prairie ecology. Drop into a dry wash and turn southwest. The sandy singletrack trail twists up the willow-filled arroyo between clay banks until it reaches a four-way trail intersection. Go left (southeast).

The next 1.3-mile trail section makes a wide loop across the southeastern part of the park to a junction north of the southern parking lot. To begin this segment, the trail quickly leaves the wash and climbs to a bench that overlooks a white badlands, with eroded hummocks of soft sandstone. Bear left here and follow the trail as it contours northeast across a basin to an eroded badlands and an old clay quarry. The trail continues uphill left of the badlands to a bench, a sign detailing human habitation of the area, and a great view west to Pikes Peak.

The trail turns southwest and gently climbs to a Y-fork trail junction at 2.4 miles. From this junction, the south parking lot is 0.1 mile to the southwest on Paint Mine Road.

To start the next 0.6-mile trail segment, which ends at the Paint Mines, hike west and reach another Y junction after a few hundred feet. Keep left on the main trail, which descends onto north-facing slopes and contours west across a shallow ravine. At 2.8 miles is a marvelous overlook above the Paint Mines. Drop down to the eastern edge of the Paint Mines to a metal bench and enjoy a view of the multicolored badlands below. Continue down the trail to the bottom of a wash and a trail junction.

Go left (south) at the junction and hike 0.2 mile up the bottom of a deep arroyo into the heart of the Paint Mines. All around you are twisted gullies, standing blocks of sandstone, hoodoos chiseled into fanciful shapes by erosion, and tumbled boulders tinted every color of the rainbow. The exposed rock here is Dawson arkose, a coarse sandstone interspersed with clay layers that was deposited fifty-five million years ago when this region was covered by a tropical hardwood forest. Don't climb on the fragile formations; they're easily damaged. Also watch your children, because there are lots of drop-offs.

Return to the intersection with the main trail and head straight (north). The last 0.7-mile trail section climbs away from the Paint Mines and returns to the trailhead. Walk north along the sandy floor of the dry arroyo for 0.2 mile to a four-way junction. Go left (west).

The last 0.5-mile of trail begins with a gradual climb up a hill to a metal bench and a good view south to the Paint Mines. Continue north on the trail as it gently descends an open grassland to a T junction. Turn left (west) and walk another 0.1 mile to reach the trailhead and parking lot.

Miles and Directions

0.0 Start at the trailhead on the east side of the parking lot (GPS: 39.020863, -104.268546) and bear left.

0.1 Go straight (east) at a trail junction onto the loop (GPS: 39.017359, -104.273012). (*Option:* Turn right to reach the Paint Mines in 0.7 mile.)

0.4 Come to an interpretive sign about prairie ecology.

1.1 Reach a four-way intersection (GPS: 39.017359, -104.268546). Go left on the loop.

1.2 Arrive at a ridge overlooking the Paint Mines.

2.4 Go right at the trail junction (GPS: 39.014091, -104.268546). (The south parking area is 0.1 mile to the left.)

2.8 Reach the trail's crest and a view of the Paint Mines.

3.0 Come to a trail junction (GPS: 39.014879, -104.269186). Turn left to reach the Paint Mines. (*Option:* A right turn here

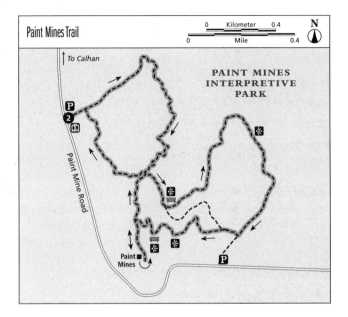

Paint Mines Trail

PAINT MINES INTERPRETIVE PARK

To Calhan

Paint Mine Road

Paint Mines

returns you directly to the trailhead.) After visiting the Paint Mines, return to the trail junction and go straight (north).

3.2 At the trail junction go left (east) uphill.

3.6 Turn left at the trail junction (GPS: 39.017213, −104.269554) to return to the trailhead.

3.7 Arrive back at the trailhead and parking lot.

3 Fountain Creek Nature Trail

This short loop hike in Fountain Creek Regional Park explores the wildlife-rich ponds and wetlands at the Cattail Marsh Wildlife Area south of Colorado Springs.

Distance: 0.6-mile loop

Hiking time: 30 minutes to 1 hour

Difficulty: Easy, with minimal elevation gain; stroller accessible when dry

Trail surface: Doubletrack dirt trail

Best season: Year-round

Other trail users: Hikers only

Canine compatibility: No dogs allowed

Fees and permits: No fees or permits required

Maps: USGS Fountain

Trail contacts: El Paso County Parks and Leisure Services, 2002 Creek Crossing, Colorado Springs, CO 80905; (719) 520-PLAY (7529); http://adm.elpasoco .com/CommunityServices/Park Operations/Pages/default.aspx Fountain Creek Nature Center, 320 Peppergrass Lane, Fountain, CO 80817; (719) 520-6745; adm.elpasoco .com/CommunityServices /RecandCulturalSvc/Pages/Foun tainCreekNatureCenter.aspx

Other: No fishing allowed

Finding the trailhead: Take I-25 south from Colorado Springs to the Mesa Ridge Parkway/CO 16 exit (exit 132). Turn left (east) at the light onto Mesa Ridge Parkway/CO 16 and drive 0.7 mile to US 85/87. Turn right (south) onto US 85/87 and drive south for 0.6 mile to a right (west) turn onto Cattail Marsh Road, marked for Fountain Creek Nature Center. Follow the dirt road to a large parking area. The trailhead is at the south side of the lot. GPS: 38.713657, -104.716642

The Hike

The Fountain Creek Nature Trail loops through the Cattail Marsh Wildlife Area along Fountain Creek. The trail explores an ecosystem of cattail-lined ponds and wetlands that offers great habitat for wildlife. The trail, accessible to strollers when dry, is mostly flat, with only slight hills at the start and finish. The year-round hike affords a much different experience from the mountain trails west of Colorado Springs.

The Cattail Marsh Wildlife Area is a lowland riparian ecosystem, one of Colorado's most species-rich habitats. The area's ponds, once gravel pits, lie on the floodplain of Fountain Creek, which begins with snowmelt on Pikes Peak and drains into the Arkansas River in Pueblo.

The wildlife area is a quiet preserve for numerous animal species and an outdoor classroom for visitors of all ages. At least 310 species of birds, mammals, reptiles, and amphibians share this habitat, including white-tailed deer, raccoon, beaver, muskrat, red fox, garter snake, bull snake, tiger salamander, painted turtle, and leopard frog. The area is also the best bird-watching site in the Pikes Peak region; more than 270 species have been spotted here. Common birds seen are red-winged blackbird, Canada goose, great blue heron, mallard and wood ducks, kingfisher, red-tailed hawk, and turkey vulture.

Start the hike at a pavilion at the south end of the parking lot and just north of the Fountain Creek Nature Center, which perches on the hill above the ponds. Inside the pavilion three interpretive signs tell about the wildlife area, Fountain Creek Regional Park, and the importance of wetlands. More signs are located along the trail. Take time to read them as you hike, and learn more about this natural area. No fishing is permitted in this protected area.

Go right on the wide trail and descend northwest down a hill to the edge of a floodplain below. At the bottom are a large picnic pavilion, a bench, and a "Walk the Wetlands" sign. The shady trail, lined with elm trees, bends left and passes a marsh. Keep alert for white-tailed deer, which often graze below the trees. The trail emerges from the woods to an open meadow filled with milkweed and a view of distant Pikes Peak.

This habitat is a designated Monarch Way Station, a stopping-off place for migrating monarch butterflies. The monarchs come in August and September when the caterpillars feed only on the white juice, or milk, of the milkweed. The plant is toxic to mammals and birds, so after feasting on the milk, the butterflies become unappetizing to birds.

After 0.2 mile the trail continues past a shallow pond lined with cattails. Stop at a shaded observation deck that juts into the pond and look for turtles and birds. The trail heads west along the northern boundary of the wildlife area, passing the pond on the left before making a left turn at a bench. Head south along the path, passing beneath elm and cottonwood trees. A large pond flanks the trail on the west, its still water reflecting trees and sky. Listen for the croak of bullfrogs or the smack of carp feeding at the pond's surface.

The trail crosses a wooden bridge, with rushing water below. Thick cattails line the path. Just past the bridge you reach a bench and a trail junction at 0.3 mile. Go left (southeast) here. (*Option:* A right turn heads west to a large pond and observation area on the far west side of the wildlife area. From there, another trail heads north 1 mile to Willow Springs Ponds.)

A massive cottonwood towers above the trail left of the junction. This gnarled tree, dubbed Grandfather Cottonwood, is one of the largest specimens in the Pikes Peak region. It's over 150 years old, as tall as a five-story building, and has a girth exceeding 20 feet at its base.

Continue southeast through open grassy glades to a large pond on the left, with willow thickets crowding its shore. This is a good spot to see red-winged blackbirds perched on cattails. Look for the brightly colored males with red and yellow stripes on their shoulders. At 0.5 mile reach a Y junction; go left (east) past a shaded bench. On your right is the Chilcott Ditch, named for early pioneer George M. Chilcott, which has carried water from Fountain Creek to nearby fields for more than one hundred years.

The hike passes the south end of a large cattail-lined pond, crossing a wooden bridge over its outlet stream. Continue east and then bend left on the trail, which swings up a dusty hill to a covered observation area. Take a minute to use the fixed binoculars here to look for great blue herons or sunning turtles in the pond below.

The last stop is the Fountain Creek Nature Center. Take the time to look around inside if you come on days that the center is open. Finish the hike at the trailhead and parking lot to the north.

Miles and Directions

0.0 Start at the trailhead at the south end of the parking area (GPS: 38.713657, -104.716642). Go right (north) on the wide trail.

0.1 Come to the Monarch Way Station.

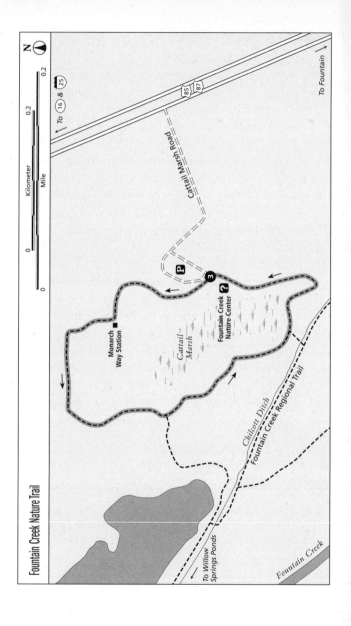

Fountain Creek Nature Trail

0.3 Go left at a trail junction (GPS: 38.713599, -104.720800).

0.5 Reach a Y junction. Go left past the south end of the pond (GPS: 38.712379, -104.717763).

0.6 Arrive back at the Fountain Creek Nature Center and the trailhead.

4 Ute Valley Park Loop

This pleasant hike, connecting several trails, explores sandstone bluffs, woods, and meadows on the northwestern edge of Colorado Springs.

Distance: 2.2-mile loop
Hiking time: 1 to 2 hours
Difficulty: Easy; 120-foot elevation gain
Trail surface: Single- and doubletrack dirt path
Best season: Year-round
Other trail users: Mountain bikers and trail runners
Canine compatibility: Leashed dogs permitted

Fees and permits: No fees or permits required
Maps: USGS Pikeview
Trail contacts: Colorado Springs Parks, Recreation, and Cultural Services, 1401 Recreation Way, Colorado Springs, CO 80905-1975; (719) 385–5940; https://coloradosprings .gov/department/76

Finding the trailhead: To reach Ute Valley Park from I-25, take the Woodman Road exit (exit 149) and turn west. Drive west on Woodman Road for 1.6 miles to Vindicator Drive. Turn right (west) onto Vindicator Drive and drive 0.7 mile. Turn left (south) into the parking lot. The trailhead is at the southeast corner of the lot. GPS: 38.924956, –104.857096

The Hike

Surrounded by suburbs in northwest Colorado Springs, Ute Valley Park is a wonderful city park with craggy bluffs and over 12 miles of trails that explore its ridges and valleys. The 541-acre park offers a quick hiking getaway with easy grades, wide trails, and plenty of solitude. Even if the parking lot is full, Ute Valley Park has plenty of room to roam.

The park harbors a foothills ecosystem, with a woodland of ponderosa pine, scrub oak, juniper, and piñon pine interspersed with wildflower-strewn meadows. The park's barebones landscape is composed of sandstone, with its main formation a long hogback on the park's west side.

When hiking in summer, watch for rattlesnakes. They're common in the park. Keep an eye on dogs and children, especially if they're scrambling around on rocks where rattlers are usually found. Other wildlife you might spot includes black bears, mountain lions, coyotes, and red foxes.

Begin your hike at the trailhead at the southeast corner of the parking lot off Vindicator Drive. Hike southeast for 120 feet past a couple benches to a trail junction. Go right on a boardwalk and walk past a cattail-lined pond; then descend southwest on a doubletrack trail across a broad meadow.

At 0.15 mile is a major Y trail junction at a ponderosa pine. Go left on a singletrack trail marked with a sign that says "Hiking Only." No mountain bikes are allowed on this next trail section. The right turn at the Y is the return trail for this hiking loop.

The next trail section, running 0.6 mile between trail junctions, heads southeast across a broad bench through a sparse ponderosa pine and scrub oak woodland interrupted by meadows and yucca. The trail gently rises then begins a long descent. A rock-rimmed canyon parallels the trail on the right.

As the trail descends, look for a social trail on the left just before the main trail drops into the main valley. Go left (east) on this side trail for 150 feet to a small sandstone arch that spans the trail. The window is 5 feet high and 6 feet wide.

Follow the trail through the arch. Do not climb on top of the arch; it's fragile and already has a crack on one side and one in the middle of the span. After viewing the arch, return to the main trail and descend south into the broad valley.

The wide trail turns southeast along the valley floor beside a deep arroyo. Follow the trail east until it divides at a Y marked with a trail sign. The shorter right-hand trail (0.15 mile) dips across the edge of the arroyo and climbs back out; the left-hand trail (0.2 mile) passes scrub oaks and reaches another trail. Go left to reach a trail junction.

Go right at this junction on a doubletrack trail and cross the arroyo on a dirt-covered culvert. Continue straight ahead (0.15 mile) to a T junction at the forest edge on the south side of the valley. Turn left (east) and hike 100 feet to a Y junction. Angle right on the sandy trail.

For the next 0.25 mile the trail heads south, slowly climbing a sandy double- to singletrack trail through a ponderosa pine forest. Stop and sniff the pines and decide if they smell like butterscotch or vanilla. Watch for mountain bikers on this segment.

Partway up the hill an old road veers left. Stay on the narrow trail to the right. At 0.2 mile from the last junction (the halfway point 1.1 miles from the trailhead), a side path heads west. Instead continue straight on the main trail for another 0.05 mile to a major junction. Go right (west) here, looking for a trail marker on the left.

The next 0.35 segment climbs west through a pine and scrub oak forest, twisting through the trees and occasionally crossing bedrock. The singletrack trail is popular with bikers. The trail emerges from the forest to an old road. Stop, catch your breath, and enjoy a great view of Pikes Peak. An alternate trailhead is located down the closed road at the end of Piñon Park Drive.

Go right (north) at the junction for the last major segment, which runs 0.55 mile north along the east side of a high hogback. The wide, rocky trail slowly climbs. At a high point, scramble right across some slabs and boulders to a flat rocky outcrop for good views across Ute Valley Park. This is a good place for a snack and drink before heading back to the main trail.

Continue hiking north on the straight trail, past a couple more viewpoints, and then descend down to a willow-lined ravine and an intermittent creek. Cross a footbridge over the creek and ascend back to the first major trail junction. Keep right and follow the trail 0.15 mile back to the parking lot.

Miles and Directions

0.0   Start at the trailhead at the southeast side of the parking lot (GPS: 38.924956, -104.857096). Go right at the junction.

0.1   Reach the first trail junction (GPS: 38.922453, -104.858190). Go left on Beaver Trail.

0.65   Follow a social trail on the left 150 feet to view an arch that spans the trail. Return to the main trail.

0.75   The trail splits. Go left.

0.8   Go right at a trail junction.

0.85   Go left at a trail junction.

0.9   Go right at a trail junction on Bear Trail (GPS: 38.915808, -104.850914).

1.1   Go straight at a trail junction.

1.15   Reach a signed trail junction (GPS: 38.913140, -104.850815). Go right on Scrub Oak Path.

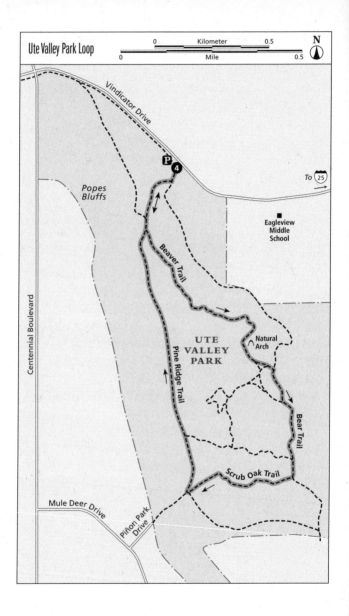

1.5	At the trail junction go right on wide Pine Ridge Trail (GPS: 38.912642, -104.856043). Enjoy a view of Pikes Peak to the southwest.
2.05	Cross a footbridge and come to a trail junction. Keep right toward the parking lot.
2.2	Arrive back at the trailhead.

Options: You can combine this loop hike with other park trails to create either longer or shorter loops. Consult the park map for details. For extra credit, climb 6,730-foot Popes Bluffs, the park's high point. To climb the bluff, hike to the first junction on this hike and head west across the valley to a trail that climbs onto the hogback. Scramble north to the summit.

5 Edna Mae Bennett Nature Trail

This excellent loop trail threads across colorful sandstone bluffs at Palmer Park in northeast Colorado Springs.

Distance: 2.6-mile loop
Hiking time: 1 to 2 hours
Difficulty: Moderate; 130-foot elevation gain
Trail surface: Single- and doubletrack dirt path
Best season: Year-round
Other trail users: Runners, cyclists, equestrians
Canine compatibility: Leashed dogs permitted

Fees and permits: No fees or permits required
Maps: USGS Pikeview
Trail contacts: Colorado Springs Parks, Recreation, and Cultural Services, 1401 Recreation Way, Colorado Springs, CO 80905-1975; (719) 385-5940; https://coloradosprings.gov/department/76 m
Other: Colorado Springs city park rules apply

Finding the trailhead: From I-25 take the Fillmore Street exit (exit 145). Drive east on Fillmore Street, which becomes North Circle Drive beyond the Union Boulevard intersection, for 2.5 miles to Paseo Road. Take a left onto Paseo Road and drive 0.8 mile northwest past the Colorado Springs Country Club golf course. Turn left immediately after passing the Palmer Park entrance; park in the lot at the North Cañon trailhead. GPS: 38.877678, –104.777601

The Hike

The Edna Mae Bennett Nature Trail is a lovely hike through the ravines and rocky bluffs of expansive Palmer Park in the urban heart of Colorado Springs. The rustic trail climbs high above the houses, affording excellent views and exploring shallow canyons, crumbling rock buttresses, and fanciful hoodoos shaped like primitive sculptures. While most Palmer Park trails are multiuse, you won't compete with mountain bikers on most of the Bennett Trail—it's too darn rocky. The trail is easy to follow, with trail markers and metal posts with arrows pointing the way.

Palmer Park, a 730-acre city park, is a rocky little wilderness surrounded by urban sprawl. This park, a wooded enclave of ponderosa pine and scrub oak, offers grand vistas of the city and the Front Range peaks.

Begin at the North Cañon parking lot on the left (north) just past the park entrance. A trail map is located on the left side of the parking area. Begin from the trailhead on the right side. Cross a wooden bridge and walk left past restrooms to a trail junction. Go right (north) on a narrow trail marked with a post on the left designating the Edna Mae Bennett Nature Trail. Hike through a copse of scrub oak and then northeast through a meadow. After 400 feet you reach a trail junction. Go left on the marked Bennett Trail.

Hike northwest and then north along the eastern edge of North Cañon, dipping through shady groves of scrub oak and passing tall pines. Across the valley to the west is the Mark Reyner Stables. After 0.5 mile the trail reaches a four-way junction of unnamed trails at a flat area that was once a parking lot. Go right on the Bennett Trail.

A large sign here dedicates the trail to the memory of Edna Mae Bennett, a schoolteacher who developed a nature-based curriculum for local children. She particularly loved to hike in the North Cañon area, so after her death in 1972, her friends built the trail to honor Bennett's legacy. Past the sign, the gently climbing path rambles along rustic split-rail fences and through a mixed woodland of ponderosa pine, juniper, and scrub oak. Climb the steepening trail, which bends east up a rocky ravine, to a switchback to the right. Just ahead is a three-way junction. Templeton Trail steps left. Go straight on the main trail.

The Bennett Trail continues slowly climbing over stone steps and timber risers as it swings across the western side of a hill above North Cañon. Above is the rocky rim of a plateau. After 0.3 mile you reach another three-way trail junction. Yucca Trail heads left. Keep straight on the Bennett Trail. Continue hiking south and then southeast. As the trail contours onto the sunny south-facing slopes, the forest thins and more views open up. Look for spectacular scenic vistas of downtown Colorado Springs to the southwest and Pikes Peak, lifting its bulky shoulders above the Front Range.

As you hike, keep alert for birds, including magpies, ravens, hawks, chickadees, pygmy nuthatches, and towhees. Palmer Park is a good bird-watching area. You'll see few animals here, however, since the city has slowly engulfed the park. You might, however, spot squirrels, rabbits, red foxes, coyotes, and an occasional rattlesnake.

After skirting the edge of North Cañon, the trail reaches its high point. Stop here and enjoy the spacious views. Pale cliffs spill down the slope below, while the city spreads west to the mountains. The trail heads southeast and begins a gentle descent as it switchbacks and traverses across the hillside. After dipping across a shallow ravine, the trail bends south and reaches a fork. Templeton Trail goes left, while the Bennett Trail heads right. Take the right fork and descend the stony trail to a short scrambling section.

A pastel-painted sandstone outcrop and amphitheater soon appears to the left, providing an excellent opportunity to catch a rest. Enjoy the scenic view from the broad ledge below cliffs, and peer into an interesting cave to the south. The small grotto corkscrews up into the cliff, forming a unique chamber that kids love to explore. This sandstone, deposited by ancient streams that flowed from the Rockies, has a rough, granular texture. The rock formation, called Dawson arkose, is soft and erodes fast.

From the trail at the north end of the amphitheater, make a sharp right hairpin turn to stay on the route. Look carefully so that you don't miss the trail and end up in the brush below. The trail rapidly descends stone stairs and steep grades in a ravine before leveling out at the base of a craggy white bluff at a three-way trail junction. Recognize the junction? You should. This is where the Edna Mae Bennett Trail splits. Take the left fork and hike 400 feet back to the trailhead.

Miles and Directions

0.0 Start at the trailhead at the North Cañon parking lot (GPS: 38.877678, -104.777601). Cross a bridge and go past the restrooms to a junction.

0.1 Go left at the junction on the Bennett Trail loop (GPS: 38.878257, -104.777159).

0.5 Reach a four-way junction at an old parking area. Go right, past the Bennett dedication sign (GPS: 38.880826, -104.778821).

1.2 Go straight at the junction with Templeton Trail (GPS: 38.881890, -104.776149).

1.7 Arrive at the trail's high point above North Cañon.

2.1 Keep right at the trail junction.

2.2 Come to an amphitheater and a cave to the left of the trail (GPS: 38.878625, -104.776006).

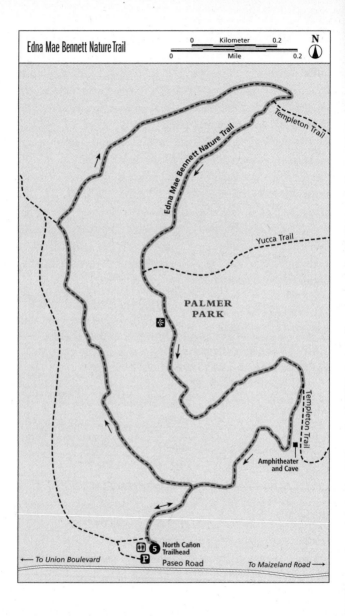

Edna Mae Bennett Nature Trail

Kilometer 0   0.2
Mile 0   0.2

N

Templeton Trail

Edna Mae Bennett Nature Trail

Yucca Trail

PALMER
PARK

Templeton Trail

Amphitheater
and Cave

North Cañon
Trailhead

Paseo Road

← To Union Boulevard

To Maizeland Road →

2.5 Return to the start of the Bennett Trail loop. Turn left at a trail junction and head downhill.

2.6 Arrive back at the trailhead and parking lot.

Options: Palmer Park boasts an extensive trail system (see the map at the parking lot) and other opportunities, including mountain biking and nature study. The park, donated to Colorado Springs by founder General William Jackson Palmer in 1902, offers more than 25 miles of trails.

6 Perkins Central Garden Trail

This short hike along a paved trail explores the heart of Garden of the Gods Park, a natural wonder of sandstone formations on the west side of Colorado Springs.

Distance: 1.3-mile lollipop
Hiking time: 30 minutes to 1 hour
Difficulty: Easy, with 25-foot elevation gain; wheelchair and stroller accessible
Trail surface: Doubletrack concrete trail
Best season: Year-round
Other trail users: Hikers only
Canine compatibility: Leashed dogs permitted

Fees and permits: No fees or permits required
Maps: USGS Cascade Quad
Trail contacts: Colorado Springs Parks, Recreation, and Cultural Services, 1401 Recreation Way, Colorado Springs, CO 80905-1975; (719) 385-5940; https://coloradosprings .gov/department/76
Other: Colorado Springs city park rules apply

Finding the trailhead: From I-25 take exit 146 and drive west on Garden of the Gods Road until it dead-ends at 30th Street against the mountain front. Turn left (south) onto 30th Street and drive south to Gateway Road, opposite the Garden of the Gods Visitor and Nature Center. Turn right (west) onto Gateway Road and follow it to Juniper Way Loop, a one-way loop road that encircles the main Garden of the Gods zone. Merge right (north) onto Juniper Way Loop and follow it to a large parking lot on the left (south) side of the road. The trailhead is at the southeast corner of the lot. GPS: 38.880937, –104.88015.

Alternatively, approach from I-25 by driving west on US 24 to 31st Street. Exit right and follow 31st Street north to a stop sign at Fillmore Street. Turn right onto Fillmore and drive 1 block. Turn left onto 30th

Street and travel north to Gateway Road. Turn left onto Gateway Road and follow the directions above to the trailhead.

The Hike

The Perkins Central Garden Trail, a paved path that loops through the central Garden zone, gets you up close and personal with the Garden of the Gods' soaring sandstone formations. The wheelchair-accessible trail has gentle gradients and plenty of scenic views. This short hike is simply one that every Colorado Springs resident and visitor should enjoy. The trail is accessible year-round, with every day and season offering new perspectives and views.

The Garden of the Gods, nestled against the Rampart Range on the west side of Colorado Springs, is an outdoor sculpture garden dominated by rock monuments. Here rise uplifted layers of sandstone that tell the geologic story of the changing earth—the uplift and erosion of mountains, periodic inundations of seas, and the coming and going of different lives.

The story of the earth from a couple billion years ago until the present can be seen at the Garden of the Gods. Few other places in the United States boast the variety and age of exposed rock found here.

Begin the trail at the southeast corner of the Main Parking Lot on the north side of the Garden off Juniper Way Loop, a one-way road that encircles the main Garden zone. A restroom and water fountain are located at the trailhead. To the right is a ramada with an interpretive display.

Hike south down the paved trail to a viewpoint surrounded by a stone wall. North Gateway Rock, also called Gate Rock, towers to the west. This huge formation, the highest in the Garden, looms 300 feet above the footpath. Continue down the trail to the Gateway, a broad opening between North Gateway Rock on the right and South Gateway Rock on the left. A couple of squat pinnacles, Red Twin and White Twin Spires, sit in the Gateway. On the right side of the trail just before the Gateway is a boulder covered with inscriptions, some dating to the nineteenth century.

A plaque on the narrow south face of North Gateway Rock details the gift of the Garden of the Gods to Colorado Springs and honors its benefactor, railroad magnate Charles Elliott Perkins. Perkins purchased the area in 1879 but allowed public visitation. Two years after Perkins's death in 1907, his children donated the land as a park that would "be kept forever open and free to the public."

At the Gateway, the trail splits. Take the left fork and hike beneath the northern edge of South Gateway Rock and past the Twin Spires on the right. A stone wall here makes a good bench for watching rock climbers on the spires. The trail curves left into the central Garden area. Follow it past South Gateway Rock on the left to Three Graces Plaza at the southern end of the paved trail. Looming above the circular plaza is 135-foot-high Montezuma Tower on the right and the narrow fins of the Three Graces.

Hike west from the plaza. (**Option:** As you descend the trail, look left for a marked dirt trail. If you want to add a scenic 0.2-mile loop to the hike, this trail climbs southeast to a rocky overlook north of Keyhole Rock. Descend back to the paved trail by continuing east through scrub oaks until it meets the main trail just east of Three Graces Plaza.)

Continue north on the Perkins trail for 0.3 mile, paralleling the park road to the left. Benches along the way allow you to sit and marvel at the rock formations. From the earliest days, the bizarre rocks have teased the imaginations of countless visitors who saw fanciful shapes, some reflected by names like Weeping Indian and Kissing Camels. Take a look across the vale and see if you can spot these two shapes. Kissing Camels is a skyline arch perched atop North Gateway. The Weeping Indian is a profile composed of white rock that faces north on the west face of South Gateway Rock.

At the north end of the Garden zone, the trail bends east, passing through thickets of scrub oak and juniper trees before emerging below the abrupt west face of North Gateway Rock. Check out an interpretive exhibit below the face, and take a moment to watch the darting flights of white-throated swifts and swallows, which nest on the rock walls.

In spring and summer you may hear the shrieking cry of a prairie falcon looking for a meal of mouse, snake, or pigeon. The falcons generally nest on the upper east face of North Gateway Rock. Another rare inhabitant of the Garden of the Gods is the honey ant, living in a handful of colonies scattered through the park.

The trail turns southeast, following below North Gateway Rock before reentering the Gateway. From here bear left and retrace your steps back on the paved trail for 0.2 mile to the trailhead and parking area.

Miles and Directions

0.0   Begin at the trailhead (GPS: 38.880937, -104.88015).

0.2   Reach the Gateway and a junction (GPS: 38.878426, -104.880322). Keep left.

0.27 Enter the central Garden zone. Keep left at a junction.

0.34 Arrive at a trail junction. Keep left toward Three Graces Plaza.

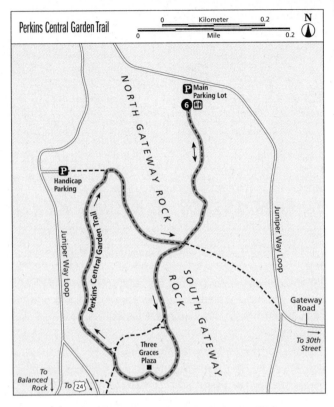

0.5 Arrive at a trail junction west of Three Graces (GPS: 38.876376, -104.882078). Keep left.

0.8 Reach another trail junction with a short trail to an accessible parking area. Keep right.

0.96 Arrive at a trail junction. Keep left on the main trail through the Gateway.

1.05 Reach a trail junction on the east side of the Gateway. Go left toward the parking area.

1.3 Arrive back at the trailhead.

7 Susan G. Bretag Trail and Palmer Trail Loop

This excellent loop hike, following four different trails, offers spectacular views of the Garden of the Gods and Pikes Peak from rocky ridges and wooded valleys.

Distance: 2.6-mile loop
Hiking time: About 1 hour
Difficulty: Moderate; 200-foot elevation gain
Trail surface: Singletrack dirt trail and doubletrack paved trail
Best season: Year-round
Other trail users: Mountain bikers and equestrians on parts of the trail
Canine compatibility: Leashed dogs permitted

Fees and permits: No fees or permits required
Maps: USGS Cascade
Trail contacts: Colorado Springs Parks, Recreation, and Cultural Services, 1401 Recreation Way, Colorado Springs, CO 80905-1975; (719) 385-5940; https://coloradosprings .gov/department/76
Other: Colorado Springs city park rules apply

Finding the trailhead: From I-25 take exit 146 and drive west on Garden of the Gods Road until it dead-ends at 30th Street against the mountain front. Turn left (south) on 30th Street and drive south to Gateway Road, opposite the Garden of the Gods Visitor and Nature Center. Turn right (west) onto Gateway Road and follow it until it merges with Juniper Way Loop, a one-way loop road that encircles the main Garden of the Gods zone. Turn right (north) on the one-way road and follow it to a large parking lot on the left. The trailhead is at the north side of the parking lot at a crosswalk. GPS: 38.872161, –104.885498

Alternatively, approach from I-25 and downtown Colorado Springs by driving west on Cimarron Street/US 24 from I-25 to Ridge Road, 0.5 mile past 31st Street. Exit right and follow Ridge Road north to a stop sign at Colorado Avenue. Cross Colorado Avenue (the road may be busy) and drive up a steep hill on Ridge Road to the Garden of the Gods. At Juniper Way Loop, go right and drive to the main parking lot on the north side of the park.

The Hike

This wonderful hike follows parts of four different trails around the main red-rock zone of the Garden of the Gods. The first section, following Palmer Trail, climbs onto ridges west of North and South Gateway Rocks before dipping down to Scotsman Picnic Area. The next segment follows Scotsman Trail back to the central Garden zone, where it picks up the paved Perkins Central Garden Trail. The last part follows the Susan G. Bretag Trail north up a broad valley east of the rock formations.

The trails are singletrack except for a wide concrete sidewalk section. Expect great views and a close-up intimate experience with the unique rock formations and the transitional ecosystems found here. Most of the trail is quiet, with few other hikers, although the section through the main Garden zone is busy. The trail also crosses the park roads four times. Be sure to use the crosswalks.

Start the hike at the trailhead on the north side of the Main Parking Lot off Juniper Way Loop. Walk north across the road to a trail junction. Go left on the Palmer Trail. The trail coming in from the right, the Susan G. Bretag Trail, is the return trail. The first trail segment on the Palmer Trail, named for General William Jackson Palmer, the founder of

Colorado Springs, runs 1.2 miles from the junction to the Scotsman Picnic Area, southwest of the central Garden zone.

Paralleling the road, the Palmer Trail goes northwest through copses of scrub oak before arcing south. It slowly gains elevation and after 0.3 mile reaches a scenic overlook. Walk 75 feet southeast off the trail for the best view and photo opportunity. All the main rock formations—North Gateway Rock, South Gateway Rock, Gray Rock, Keyhole Rock, Montezuma Ruins, and the Three Graces—tower to the south, their ragged outlines etched against the sky.

Past the overlook, the trail turns west and contours through a shallow canyon before climbing onto east-facing slopes opposite North Gateway Rock, the park's highest formation. The trail continues climbing through a piñon pine and juniper woodland until it reaches a high point and then descends to a shoulder. This is another great view-point. Note the Kissing Camels, a small arch perched atop North Gateway Rock on the left, and the Weeping Indian, the white rock profile of an Indian face on South Gateway Rock. Continue south down the trail and reach a junction 0.8 mile from the trailhead. From here a short trail heads left to the central Garden zone. Stay straight on the Palmer Trail, ignoring another side trail that jogs over to the road 100 feet farther down.

The Palmer Trail passes beneath the west face of the Giant Footprints, a couple of tilted slabs composed of 220-million-year-old Fountain Formation sandstone, and then descends southwest parallel to the park road through scrub oak for 0.4 mile. When the trail reaches the edge of the road at 1.2 miles, you're opposite the Scotsman Picnic Area. Cross the road to a parking lot and cross a bridge. A restroom, open in summer only, is to your left. Go right on the Scotsman Trail.

Follow the Scotsman Trail northeast for 0.4 mile. The sandy trail, often used by horses, slowly climbs. At an obvious junction, keep left and hike to Juniper Way Loop road. Cross the road just north of a parking area and follow a trail into the central Garden zone.

The next 0.5 mile of trail follows the paved Perkins Central Garden Trail, the Garden's most popular trail. Hike north and then east on the paved path, passing north of the Three Graces and Montezuma Tower, both slender spires popular with rock climbers. At an obvious T junction, go left (north) and hike to the Gateway, the huge gap between North and South Gateway Rocks. At the trail junction here below the dedication plaque, go right on a paved trail and walk 0.15 mile east to Juniper Way Loop.

The last trail segment follows the Susan G. Bretag Trail for 0.5 mile back to the trailhead and parking lot. Cross the road at a crosswalk and turn left onto the marked trail. Follow the wide trail north in a valley between rock formations on the west and a hogback to the east. The trail crosses a meadow covered with grass and yucca. After 0.3 mile it reaches a Y junction with the Dakota Trail. Keep left and follow the Susan G. Bretag Trail, which bends northwest. End your hike at the start of the Palmer Trail. Cross the road back to the trailhead. If you're thirsty or need the facilities, a water fountain and restrooms are located on the southeast side of the parking lot.

Miles and Directions

0.0 Start at the trailhead on the north side of the main Garden parking lot (GPS: 38.872161, -104.885498). Cross the road to a T junction and turn left (west) onto the Palmer Trail.

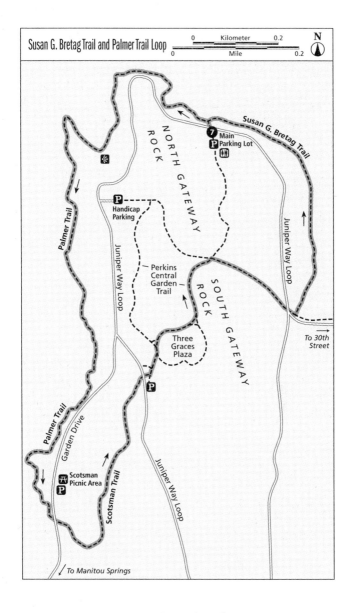

Susan G. Bretag Trail and Palmer Trail Loop

N

Kilometer
0   0.2
Mile
0   0.2

Susan G. Bretag Trail

NORTH GATEWAY ROCK

7 Main Parking Lot

Juniper Way Loop

P Handicap Parking

Juniper Way Loop

Perkins Central Garden Trail

SOUTH GATEWAY ROCK

To 30th Street

Three Graces Plaza

Palmer Trail

Garden Drive

Scotsman Picnic Area

Scotsman Trail

Juniper Way Loop

Palmer Trail

To Manitou Springs

0.3 Come to a scenic overlook on the left (GPS: 38.881298, –104.883461).

0.8 Reach a junction with a short trail to the Garden zone on the left (GPS: 38.877218, –104.884248). Go straight.

1.2 Reach a road opposite the Scotsman Picnic Area (GPS: 38.872161, –104.884861). Cross the road to the left and then cross a bridge to reach Scotsman Trail. Go right.

1.6 End the Scotsman Trail at Juniper Way Loop road (GPS: 38.87569, –104.88253). Cross the road to the central Garden zone. Follow the trail straight to the paved Perkins Central Garden Trail.

2.1 End the Perkins Central Garden Trail at the Juniper Way Loop on the east side of the park (GPS: 38.877193, –104.878011). Cross the street and turn left (north) onto the Susan G. Bretag Trail.

2.6 End the Susan G. Bretag Trail at the junction with the Palmer Trail. Go left across the road to arrive back at the trailhead and parking lot.

8 Ridge Trail

A short lollipop loop trail with great views follows a ridge in the southern sector of the Garden of the Gods.

Distance: 0.37-mile lollipop
Hiking time: About 30 minutes
Difficulty: Easy; minimal elevation gain
Trail surface: Singletrack dirt path
Best season: Year-round
Other trail users: Hikers only
Canine compatibility: Leashed dogs permitted
Fees and permits: No fees or permits required

Maps: USGS Cascade
Trail contacts: Colorado Springs Parks, Recreation, and Cultural Services, 1401 Recreation Way, Colorado Springs, CO 80905-1975; (719) 385-5940; https://coloradosprings .gov/department/76
Other: Colorado Springs city park rules apply

Finding the trailhead: From I-25 take exit 146 and drive west on Garden of the Gods Road until it dead-ends at 30th Street against the mountain front. Turn left (south) onto 30th Street and drive south to Gateway Road, opposite the Garden of the Gods Visitor and Nature Center. Turn right (west) onto Gateway Road and follow it until it merges with Juniper Way Loop, a one-way loop road that encircles the main Garden of the Gods zone. Turn right (north) onto the one-way road; follow it past a large parking lot on the left and completely around the main Garden zone to the South Garden parking lot on the right. The trailhead is at the north side of the parking lot just west of a ramada. GPS: 38.870105, -104.878227

Alternatively, approach from I-25 and downtown Colorado Springs by driving west on Cimarron Street/US 24 from I-25 to Ridge Road,

0.5 mile past 31st Street. Exit right and follow Ridge Road north to a stop sign at Colorado Avenue. Cross Colorado Avenue and drive up Ridge Road to the Garden of the Gods. At the one-way Juniper Way Loop road, go right and drive to the South Garden parking lot on the right. The trailhead is at the north side of the parking lot, west of a ramada.

The Hike

The easy Ridge Trail, a local favorite, ascends to a scenic overlook atop a ridge before circling back to the trailhead. The singletrack trail has a good surface, gradual grades, and marvelous views of Keyhole Rock and Gray Rock in the southern part of the Garden of the Gods. The popular trail is for hikers only; no mountain bikes or horses are permitted.

Begin the hike from the parking area south of a ramada at the South Garden Parking Lot on the east side of Juniper Way Loop road in the southeastern sector of Garden of the Gods Park. Cross the road at a crosswalk and hike northwest on the wide trail for 0.06 mile up a broad slope to a trail junction. Go right on the singletrack trail. The next trail section, a 0.25-mile loop, returns you to this junction.

The trail climbs past a switchback onto the crest of a rocky ridge. Hike north to an overlook perched above a shallow canyon to the north. Gray Rock, towering on the canyon's east side, is composed of whitish Lyons sandstone. Keyhole Rock is the long sandstone fin flanking the west side. Don't scramble onto either rock without proper climbing equipment or registering at the visitor center as a rock climber. Keyhole Rock is one of the park's most dangerous formations, since it's easier to climb up than down. It's

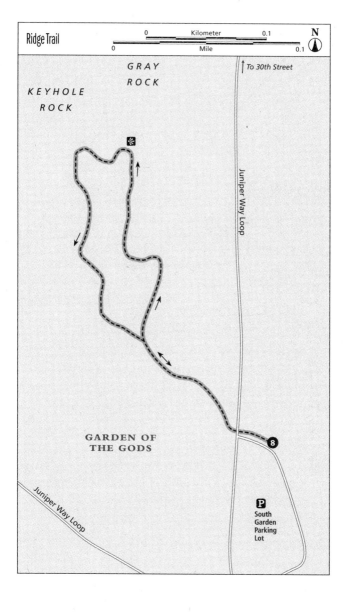

Ridge Trail

Kilometer
0   0.1
Mile
0   0.1

N

GRAY
ROCK

To 30th Street

KEYHOLE
ROCK

Juniper Way Loop

GARDEN OF
THE GODS

8

Juniper Way Loop

P
South
Garden
Parking
Lot

composed of salmon-colored Lyons sandstone, deposited as sand dunes almost 280 million years ago.

The trail winds down the west side of the ridge on bedrock before making a sharp left turn. Hike south along the west side of the ridge. Look west for great views of Pikes Peak and the southern ridge of Keyhole Rock. When you reach the trail fork at the base of the ridge, continue straight to the trailhead and parking area.

Miles and Directions

0.0   Start at the trailhead at a ramada on the north end of the South Garden Parking Lot (GPS: 38.870105, -104.878227). Follow a trail next to the exit road for 60 feet to a crosswalk. Cross a road and follow the trail northwest.

0.06   Go right at a junction with the loop trail (GPS: 38.870842, -104.879452).

0.1   Reach a viewpoint that looks north to Gray Rock (GPS: 38.871390, -104.879177).

0.3   Reach a junction at the end of the loop. Go straight to the parking lot.

0.37   Arrive back at the trailhead and parking lot.

9 Siamese Twins Trail

This lovely trail leads you through shallow canyons in the Garden of the Gods to a scenic vista amid sandstone pillars.

Distance: 0.55-mile loop

Hiking time: 30 minutes to 1 hour

Difficulty: Easy; 108-foot elevation gain

Trail surface: Dirt path

Best season: Year-round

Other trail users: Equestrians

Canine compatibility: Leashed dogs permitted

Fees and permits: No fees or permits required

Schedule: Park open 5 a.m. to 11 p.m. May 1 to Oct 31; 5 a.m. to 9 p.m. Nov 1 to Apr 30

Maps: USGS Manitou Springs

Trail contacts: Colorado Springs Parks, Recreation, and Cultural Services, 1401 Recreation Way, Colorado Springs, CO 80905-1975; (719) 385-5940; https://coloradosprings .gov/department/76

Finding the trailhead: Take the Cimarron (US 24 West) exit from I-25 and drive west for 2.6 miles. Turn right onto 31st Street and then left onto Colorado Avenue after 1 block. Drive west on Colorado to a right turn on Beckers Lane, which leads to the Garden of the Gods Trading Post. Here you veer right onto Garden Lane. Take the first left to continue on Garden Drive. Turn right into the Spring Canyon trailhead parking lot. The trail begins in the northwest corner of the lot, where you will also find a map of area trails. GPS: 38.868234, –104.890359

The Hike

The Garden of the Gods, the most famous natural wonder near Colorado Springs, needs to be at the top of every hiker's must-see list. A variety of hiking trails explores this spectacular city park. The Siamese Twins Trail, one of the area's less-traveled easy hikes, offers an excellent opportunity to get off the beaten path in the southwest sector of the park.

The hike begins at a marked trailhead at the northwest corner of the parking lot. Walk north along a split-rail fence, passing the Cabin Canyon Trail junction on the left. Stay right, following a trail marker and climbing occasional steps.

The trail follows a sandstone arroyo through a pygmy forest of scrub oak, piñon pine, and juniper. The Fountain Formation sandstone, a thick layer of sedimentary rock tilted up against the mountains, was deposited along the eastern edge of the Ancestral Rocky Mountains about 300 million years ago. Notice its coarse composition of pebbles and cobbles, which were washed off the mountains and deposited in broad alluvial fans along the edge of an ancient sea.

A second set of stairs leads to a dry streambed, which you ford by a dirt bridge built on a culvert. As the trail continues, sandstone formations appear above spiny yucca and twisted juniper trees. The trail circles southeast toward the Siamese Twins, two conjoined pinnacles. Clamber up left behind the spires (GPS: 38.869957, −104.888472) at a trail marker (0.3 mile) to a marvelous viewpoint. To the south rise the sandstone humps of Red Rock Canyon, with Cheyenne Mountain and the Front Range looming in the distance. You will find an interesting and unique view of Pikes Peak through an eroded window at the base of the Siamese Twins, providing a wonderful photo opportunity in morning light.

To descend back to the trailhead and parking lot, circle around to the west side of the Twins; rejoin the trail at a marker and go left (south). Pass a second trail marker at the base of a great slab of red rock, and hike beside a log fence.

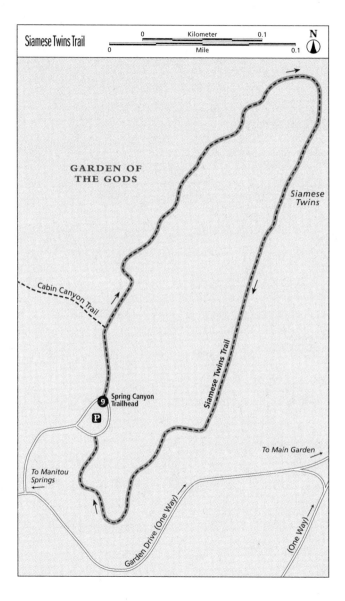

Siamese Twins Trail

GARDEN OF
THE GODS

Siamese
Twins

Cabin Canyon Trail

Spring Canyon
Trailhead

9

P

To Main Garden

To Manitou
Springs

Siamese Twins Trail

Garden Drive (One Way)

(One Way)

Kilometer

0   0.1

Mile

0   0.1

N

The winding path takes you down the spine of a ridge, then along a second log fence to another trail marker. Turn right (west) here. The park road is visible to your left. From here it's a quick hop (0.25 mile) down some stairs to the parking lot.

Miles and Directions

0.0 Begin at the trailhead on the north side of parking lot (GPS: 38.868234, -104.890359). Walk the trail clockwise.

0.3 Reach the Siamese Twins (GPS: 38.869957, -104.888472).

0.55 Arrive back at the trailhead on the south side of parking lot.

10 Red Mountain Trail

This short hike, initially following the Intemann Trail, climbs to the summit of 7,361-foot Red Mountain, where you'll find commanding views of Manitou Springs and Pikes Peak.

Distance: 3 miles out and back
Hiking time: 1 to 2 hours
Difficulty: Moderate; 800-foot elevation gain
Trail surface: Doubletrack and singletrack dirt trail
Best season: Mar through Nov; icy in winter
Other trail users: Hikers only
Canine compatibility: Dogs permitted

Fees and permits: No fees or permits required
Maps: USGS Manitou Springs
Trail contacts: Manitou Springs Public Services Department, 606 Manitou Ave., Manitou Springs, CO 80829; (719) 685-5481; www.manitousspringsgov.com/gov ernment/departments/planning /post

Finding the trailhead: The hike begins at the Iron Springs trailhead by Iron Springs Chateau in Manitou Springs. From Colorado Springs drive west on US 24 and take the first exit for Manitou Avenue. Drive west on Manitou Avenue to a roundabout and turn left onto Ruxton Avenue, following signs for the Pikes Peak Cog Railway. Follow Ruxton until it splits into a one-way road to the cog railway depot and a one-way street back to Manitou Avenue. Go right and follow the road to the depot; make a U-turn left onto the return one-way street. Find a paid parking place to park here or along the right side of Ruxton Avenue. Parking is problematic in summer. It's best to park at a free lot at 10 Old Man's Trail on the east side of Manitou, and take a free shuttle between 6 a.m. and 6 p.m. to the trailhead. The Iron Springs trailhead for the Paul Intemann Memorial Nature Trail is on the right, just before Ruxton becomes a two-way street. GPS: 38.857289, -104.927498

The Hike

Red Mountain, a low peak rising above Manitou Springs, offers a great hike to some of the area's best views. Despite the mountain's steep slopes, the trail wends to the peak's 7,361-foot summit with gradual grades that switchback across the steepest slopes. Besides fun hiking and great views, Red Mountain offers a surprise ending—the remains of a restaurant, casino, and summit house of an incline railway.

Begin your adventure at the Iron Springs trailhead next to Ruxton Avenue below the Pikes Peak Cog Railroad station and the Iron Springs Chateau. After finding a parking spot on either Ruxton Avenue or Iron Springs Road, which can be a problem during the busy summer tourist season, hike east on a trail along the south side of Ruxton Creek past the Iron Springs, a mineral spring under a pavilion on the north bank of the creek. Continue down the trail to Spring Road and go right onto the road.

Walk up the dirt road to a gate, and pass onto the Intemann Trail. The first 0.5-mile segment of this hike follows the Paul Intemann Memorial Nature Trail, a trail that contours east above Manitou Springs. The trail is named for Paul Intemann, a Manitou Springs city planner who envisioned a network of trails above Manitou. He died in a car accident in New Mexico in 1986.

Follow the closed road up a draw, around a blunt ridge, and up a broad vale toward a couple of power poles. Look to the right before the poles for a sign marking the start of the Red Mountain Trail. This 1-mile spur trail, built by volunteers in 1999 and 2001, is on a swath of Manitou Springs Open Space land.

Turn right (south) and hike up the Red Mountain Trail, which slowly climbs southwest in a mixed conifer forest of ponderosa pine and Douglas fir left of a steep ravine. Follow the trail as it switchbacks up the steep slope until it swings left and climbs to a saddle on a ridge. This is the official end of the trail but not the hike.

Go left at the saddle and continue up the rocky trail, which threads above the steep eastern flank of Red Mountain. After climbing 50 feet, the trail ends on the mountain's flat summit.

The summit of 7,361-foot-high Red Mountain offers wonderful views. Below nestles Manitou Springs, with houses lining its hilly roads. The distant sounds of traffic, barking dogs, and music filter upward. To the east rise the red rocks of Garden of the Gods, and beyond spreads the prairie horizon. The westward view is spectacular. Pikes Peak rears high above. Lower, the pinnacles Gog and Magog perch on a long ridge.

The top of Red Mountain, however, is not just about views. If you look around, you'll see the concrete foundations of several buildings erected here in the early twentieth century. The Red Mountain Incline Railway ferried visitors up the mountain's steep northeast face. The lower concrete footings mark where the railway ended and visitors disembarked. The upper foundations mark the former site of a restaurant, bar, and dance hall, where both live music and whiskey flowed. Some even say it was a casino and a gentlemen's club—a polite way of saying it was a brothel—but that's just rumor.

Before the railway, Red Mountain's summit was a gravesite. In the nineteenth century, Manitou Springs was a healing place for tuberculosis patients, who came for the

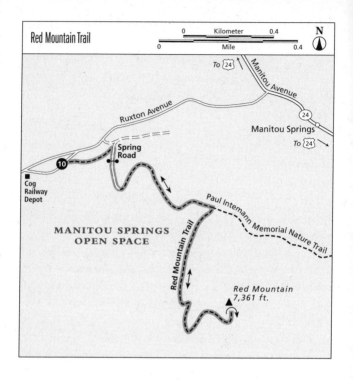

Red Mountain Trail

0 Kilometer 0.4
0 Mile 0.4

N

To 24
Manitou Avenue
Ruxton Avenue
Manitou Springs
To 24
10
Spring Road
Cog Railway Depot
Paul Intemann Memorial Nature Trail
MANITOU SPRINGS OPEN SPACE
Red Mountain Trail
Red Mountain 7,361 ft.

dry air and healing springs. Young Emma Crawford came for the cure in 1889 but died in 1891 at the age of 19. She once hiked to the summit, where she had a vision and left a scarf tied on a tree by her chosen burial plot. After Emma's death, her fiancé and twelve pallbearers carried her coffin up Red Mountain and buried her on top. In 1912 the coffin was moved to the south so that the summit house could be built. After heavy rains in 1929, Emma's coffin washed down the mountain, spilling her remains. She was reburied in a Manitou cemetery, but many locals say that her ghost stalks Red Mountain and some have seen the Victorian-clad specter. Every October, Manitou Springs hosts a coffin race in her honor.

After brooding on the summit about this history, turn around and retrace your steps 1.5 miles back down the trail to the trailhead.

Miles and Directions

0.0   Start at the Iron Springs trailhead for the Paul Intemann Memorial Nature Trail (GPS: 38.857289, -104.927498).

0.1   Go right at the junction with Spring Road.

0.15   Come to a junction with a road. Pass through a gate and go right on the Intemann Trail.

0.5   Go right at the junction with Red Mountain Trail.

1.5   Reach the summit of Red Mountain, your turnaround point (GPS: 38.8514, -104.9212).

2.5   Return to the junction with the Intemann Trail. Go left.

3.0   Arrive back at the trailhead.

11 Lower Barr Trail

Barr Trail climbs 13 miles to the summit of Pikes Peak, but this great day hike follows the trail's first 3 miles up Mount Manitou to wonderful views of the surrounding mountains.

Distance: 6.4 miles out and back

Hiking time: 3 to 5 hours

Difficulty: Moderate; 1,600-foot elevation gain

Trail surface: Wide singletrack dirt path

Best season: Year-round; cold and icy in winter

Other trail users: Runners

Canine compatibility: Leashed dogs permitted

Fees and permits: No fees or permits required

Maps: USGS Manitou Springs

Trail contacts: Pike National Forest, Pikes Peak Ranger District, 601 South Weber St., Colorado Springs, CO 80903; (719) 636-1602; www.fs.usda.gov

Finding the trailhead: To reach the Barr trailhead from I-25, take the Cimarron Street/US 24 exit and drive west on US 24 for 5.4 miles to the first Manitou Springs exit. The exit ramp circles onto Manitou Avenue. Turn right and drive west on Manitou Avenue for 1.4 miles (following signs for the cog railroad) to a roundabout at its intersection with Ruxton Avenue. Turn left (southwest) at the roundabout onto Ruxton and travel 0.8 mile, past the cog railroad depot to Hydro Street. Turn right (northwest) onto Hydro Street and drive uphill 0.1 mile to the parking area and trailhead. (**Note:** The parking lot is usually full, especially in the morning. If it is, paid parking is found on Ruxton Avenue below the cog railroad depot. Do not park in the cog railroad parking lots. Parking is a big problem in summer. It's best to park at a free lot at 10 Old Man's Trail on the east side of Manitou and take a free shuttle between 6 a.m. and 6 p.m. to the trailhead.) GPS: 38.855768, –104.933923

The Hike

Pikes Peak, looming 8,000 feet above Colorado Springs, is one of America's most famous mountains. The summit of the 14,115-foot peak is reached by auto road, cog railroad, and the Barr Trail, which climbs 12.6 miles from Manitou Springs to the summit. Barr Trail, while a difficult hike up Colorado's thirty-first highest peak, is not an easy day hike. Instead, do this shorter, 6.4-mile round-trip hike up the trail's lower section and sample some of its best terrain and views.

This hike, switchbacking up the eastern face of 9,250-foot Rocky Mountain, a spur of Mount Manitou, features easy grades on the wide trail, fabulous views, and moderate hiking. Take your time and plenty of rest breaks, especially if you aren't accustomed to the altitude, and you will be fine. Wear sturdy shoes, maintain a steady pace, and carry water and energy drinks in summer. At the top you'll be rewarded for your efforts.

Begin the hike at the trailhead at a parking area on Hydro Street. Hike up switchbacks on the trail, which traverses back and forth across the mountain's east face above Englemann Canyon to the south. After 0.3 mile you reach a trail junction. Bend sharply right on Barr Trail. As you slowly climb through scrub oak, ponderosa pine, and Douglas fir, great views unfold of Manitou Springs below, the red rocks of Garden of the Gods to the northeast, and sprawling Colorado Springs beyond. Hiking up Barr Trail from Manitou Springs to the summit is like taking a telescoped journey from Mexico to the Arctic, passing through almost all the major ecological life zones.

A trail marker at 1 mile designates your elevation as 7,200 feet. Past here, large granite boulders line the trail. You pass a lofty rock outcrop at 1.8 miles that offers spectacular views of

Englemann Canyon to the south. This is a good picnic spot and, if you're tired, a turnaround point.

Barr Trail continues west, alternately traversing steep slopes and climbing switchbacks up the south-facing side of Rocky Mountain. Rocky slopes spill into the canyon, and if you look closely you'll spot the tracks of the cog railroad below. Farther along, the trail ducks through a tunnel of boulders that have fallen against one another like giant dominos and passes a small tunnel on the right. At 2.6 miles you reach a trail junction at No Name Creek. To finish the hike, go right on Eagle's Nest Trail, sometimes called the Incline Trail. (Barr Trail continues straight west from the junction, toward Barr Camp and the Pikes Peak summit.)

Follow the flat, wide Incline Trail east past a granite cliff to a trail fork. Go left (east) on the upper trail, which heads slightly downhill to the Eagle's Nest Trail sign at 3 miles. Keep right (east) on the descending trail to a stunning overlook and the hike's turnaround point at Eagle's Nest Picnic Area (3.2 miles) and the top of the Manitou Incline Trail, sometimes called America's toughest trail. From this lofty perch you'll enjoy an eagle's view of the city below, spreading east to the tawny prairie and the distant horizon.

Catch your breath, take a drink of water, and rest your feet for a few minutes. Now tighten your boot laces and head back the way you came. The return trip, all of it downhill, goes fast. Remember the trail junctions on the way down. Stick to the well-beaten trail, and you'll be fine.

Miles and Directions

0.0 Start at the Barr Trail trailhead at the parking area on Hydro Street (GPS: 38.855768, -104.933923).

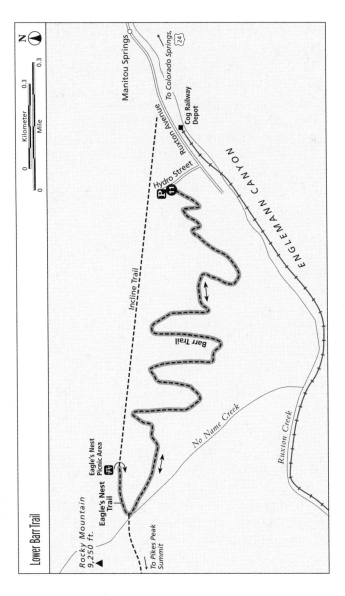

Lower Barr Trail

Rocky Mountain 9,250 ft.

To Pikes Peak Summit

Eagle's Nest Picnic Area

Eagle's Nest Trail

No Name Creek

Incline Trail

Barr Trail

Hydro Street

Ruxton Creek

ENGLEMANN CANYON

Manitou Springs

Ruxton Avenue

Cog Railway Depot

To Colorado Springs, 24

N

0   Kilometer   0.3

0   Mile   0.3

0.3 At the junction go right on the main trail.

1.0 Pass the 7,200-foot elevation marker.

1.8 Rest at the overlook rocks. (***Option:*** Turn around here for a 3.6-mile round-trip hike.)

2.6 Reach the Eagle's Nest Trail intersection (GPS: 38.856427, –104.954929). Go right on the Eagle's Nest Trail.

3.2 Arrive at the Eagle's Nest Picnic Area (GPS: 38.858432, –104.947980) on top of the Manitou Incline Trail. Retrace your steps back to Barr Trail.

6.4 Arrive back at the trailhead.

12 Red Rock Canyon Trail

A classic hike flanked by towering sandstone walls follows an old road in the heart of Red Rock Canyon Open Space.

Distance: 2.2 miles out and back

Hiking time: 1 to 2 hours

Difficulty: Easy; 150-foot elevation gain

Trail surface: Doubletrack dirt path

Best season: Year-round

Other trail users: Runners, mountain bikers, equestrians

Canine compatibility: Leashed dogs permitted

Fees and permits: No fees or permits required

Maps: USGS Manitou Springs; trail map available at park website

Trail contacts: Colorado Springs Parks, Recreation, and Cultural Services, 1401 Recreation Way, Colorado Springs, CO 80905-1975; (719) 385-5940; https://coloradosprings .gov/department/76

Finding the trailhead: Red Rock Canyon Open Space is directly south of Garden of the Gods and US 24. To access the area from downtown Colorado Springs and I-25, take the Cimarron Street/US 24 exit (exit 141) and drive west about 3.5 miles toward the mountains. Access the parking areas and trailheads by turning left (south) on South Ridge Road from US 24, which is the only left turn between 31st Street and the first Manitou Springs exit. Use extreme caution turning on and off the busy highway. Drive south on South Ridge Road for 0.1 mile and turn left into the park. Drive through a roundabout and go left. Park at the first parking area. (***Note:*** Portable toilets and a map are located at the trailhead at the east end of the lot. Additional parking is available at a lot at the end of the park road to the southeast.) GPS: 38.853326, –104.879251

The Hike

The Red Rock Canyon Trail explores Red Rock Canyon, the centerpiece of 1,474-acre Red Rock Canyon Open Space. The city of Colorado Springs purchased the park's initial 787 acres in 2003, saving the area from trophy homes, a golf course, and resort development. Red Rock Canyon itself is a mile-long canyon lined with ruddy sandstone cliffs and floored by scrub oak, cottonwood trees, and grassy meadows. In addition to its natural beauty and dramatic geology, the canyon harbors archaeological and historical sites, including a stone quarry that operated from 1886 through 1915.

Begin the hike from the trailhead at the east side of the main parking lot, located on the north side of the park opposite US 24. Portable toilets and a trail map are at the trailhead. An alternative parking area is located past the first parking area at the end of the park road below Red Rock Canyon. If you park here, knock 0.4 mile off your hike.

The first trail segment runs east and then south for 0.35 mile before joining an old road. Just east of the trailhead is a junction with the Mesa and Greenlee Trails, which head south up a closed road. Continue straight and pass the left side of a free-ride biking area. Past here the wide trail bends south. Follow the trail between the south parking area and a sandstone cliff that was quarried in the nineteenth century. The trail slowly climbs and then bends east to join the old Red Rock Canyon road. (If you started from the south parking area, it's 0.15 mile to this point.)

Hike up the road 0.1 mile, passing a locked gate, to the site of the old Bock house, now a picnic and rest pavilion. Red Rock Canyon once belonged to John George Bock, who assembled the house during the 1920s and 1930s. He started with a tourist camp and stables and slowly bought other land from stone companies and for back taxes.

After Bock's death, his two sons, John and Richard, wanted to build a World Trade Center here with golf courses, luxury homes and condos, a shopping center, office buildings, a sports arena, and thirteen lakes. They were unable to get the area rezoned, so in the 1970s it was turned into a landfill and gravel pit. In the 1990s another developer attempted to resurrect the Bock plan but was denied annexation by both Manitou Springs and Colorado Springs, leaving the door open for its purchase as parkland.

The next trail section follows the old road on the east side of the canyon for 0.4 mile to its junction with Quarry Pass Trail.

The last trail segment continues south for 0.25 mile on the old road, steadily climbing a hill to a major junction and the hike's turnaround point at 6,400 feet. Take a minute and enjoy the view. Directly west across the wooded canyon is the Wiggins Wall, named for famed local climber Earl Wiggins, and a deep defile called Black Bear Canyon. This and the other cliffs in Red Rock Canyon are popular with rock climbers, who enjoy more than one hundred established climbing routes. From this high point, retrace the trail north to the parking lot, following either Red Rock Canyon Trail or Red Rock Canyon Path from the Quarry Pass Trail Junction to the pavilion at the pond.

Miles and Directions

0.0   Begin at the trailhead at the east end of the main parking lot (GPS: 38.853326, -104.879251).

0.35   Reach a junction with a closed dirt road (GPS: 38.84971, -104.879644).

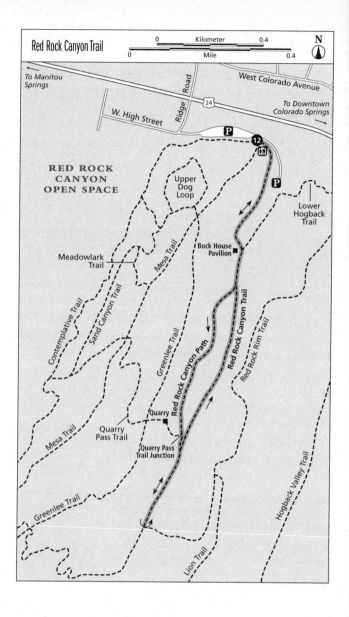

0.45   Reach the pavilion and lake (GPS: 38.848932, -104.880134).

0.85   Arrive at the junction with Quarry Pass Trail (GPS: 38.843297, -104.882469). Go straight.

1.1   End the first half of your hike at the top of a hill at a three-way trail junction with Red Rock Rim Trail (GPS: 38.840008, -104.884362). Turn around and hike back north toward the trailhead.

2.2   Arrive back at the trailhead.

Option 1: For an alternative hike, go right at the pavilion and descend stone steps to a small lake. Bear right and follow the singletrack 0.5-mile Red Rock Canyon Path, a hiker-only trail, along the west side of the canyon to the Quarry Pass Trail Junction.

For a diversion, go right at the Quarry Pass Trail Junction at 0.85 mile and follow the Quarry Pass Trail 0.1 mile up to the nineteenth-century stone quarry, a historic site. The sandstone blocks quarried here were loaded on train cars on a railroad spur that ran into the canyon and then shipped to Denver, Kansas, and Texas. The stone, however, didn't weather well, and the canyon's quarries closed by 1915. This side trail climbs to the quarry. Make sure you climb the stone staircase into the quarry. After visiting the quarry, retrace your steps back to the main trail at Quarry Pass Trail Junction.

Option 2: Several excellent loop hikes fan out from the end of the Red Rock Canyon Trail. The best hike continues south up the canyon for 0.15 mile before turning west up a deep canyon. Follow the 1.3-mile Roundup Trail up and out of the canyon; then dip across the heads of a couple shallow canyons before descending north to the southern end of the Contemplative Trail. This 3.5-mile loop hike is an excellent easy day hike.

13 Contemplative Trail to Sand Canyon Trail Loop

This excellent and peaceful loop hike wanders through soaring sandstone formations in the western sector of Red Rock Canyon Open Space.

Distance: 1.6-mile loop
Hiking time: 1 to 2 hours
Difficulty: Easy; 150-foot elevation gain
Trail surface: Singletrack dirt path
Best season: Year-round
Other trail users: Hikers only
Canine compatibility: Leashed dogs permitted
Fees and permits: No fees or permits required

Maps: USGS Manitou Springs; trail map available at park website
Trail contacts: Colorado Springs Parks, Recreation, and Cultural Services, 1401 Recreation Way, Colorado Springs, CO 80905-1975; (719) 385-5940; https://coloradosprings .gov/department/76

Finding the trailhead: Red Rock Canyon Open Space is directly south of Garden of the Gods and US 24. To access the area from downtown Colorado Springs and I-25, take the Cimarron Street/ US 24 exit (exit 141) and drive west about 3.5 miles toward the mountains. Access the parking areas and trailheads by turning left (south) onto South Ridge Road from US 24, which is the only left turn between 31st Street and the first Manitou Springs exit. Use extreme caution turning on and off the busy highway. Drive south on South Ridge Road for 0.1 mile and turn left into the park. Drive through a roundabout and go left. The trailhead is located at the western end of the first parking lot. GPS: 38.853554, –104.881362

The Hike

The 0.55-mile Contemplative Trail coupled with 0.9 mile of the 1.6-mile-long Sand Canyon Trail forms a wonderful loop hike on the west side of Red Rock Canyon Open Space. The hike wanders through soaring fins of sandstone, thickets of scrub oak, ponderosa pine woods, and flower-strewn meadows. The Contemplative Trail section is open to hikers only. Several benches scattered along the quiet trail allow contemplation. Keep an eye out for wildlife, including mule deer and black bears, in the valley below the trail. The return hike on Sand Canyon Trail parallels the same rock formations on their east side.

Start the hike at the parking lot on the north side of the park. Portable toilets and an open space trail map are located at the east end of the lot. The trailhead is located at the lot's west end.

Hike west from the trailhead to an old road. After 100 feet make a left turn onto the singletrack Sand Canyon Trail. The trail climbs south below a spectacular sandstone fin. Reach a trail junction 0.25 mile from the trailhead. The Contemplative Trail begins here. Go straight.

The hikers-only Contemplative Trail twists south, passing beneath tall rock formations, dipping through shallow vales, and climbing short hills. One spectacular section squeezes through a rock-walled passageway. At its end, the trail climbs timber steps and ends on Sand Canyon Trail, an old road. Go left (east) on Sand Canyon Trail.

Alternatively, you can go straight across the four-way intersection and follow the Roundup Trail for 1.1 miles to the top of Red Rock Canyon and return down Red Rock Canyon Trail.

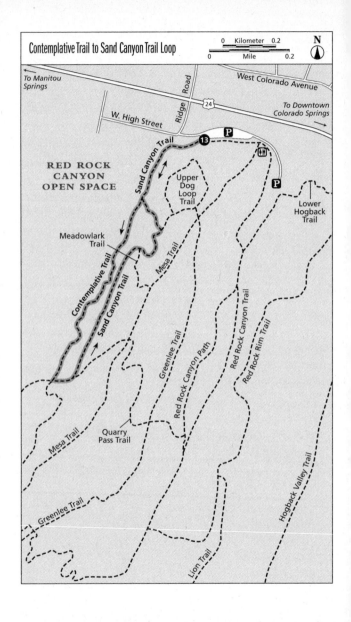

0   Kilometer   0.2

0   Mile   0.2

N

To Manitou
Springs

West Colorado Avenue

Ridge Road

24

W. High Street

To Downtown
Colorado Springs

13

P

P

RED ROCK
CANYON
OPEN SPACE

Sand Canyon Trail

Upper
Dog
Loop
Trail

Lower
Hogback
Trail

Meadowlark
Trail

Contemplative Trail

Mesa Trail

Sand Canyon Trail

Mesa Trail

Greenlee Trail

Quarry
Pass Trail

Red Rock Canyon Path

Red Rock Canyon Trail

Red Rock Rim Trail

Greenlee Trail

Hogback Valley Trail

Lion Trail

Sand Canyon Trail bends north at a junction with Quarry Pass Trail. Stay left on the main trail and hike north on the doubletrack trail for 0.4 mile to a junction with Meadowlark Trail. This trail segment follows the old road parallel to a series of tilted rock slabs called the Ironing Boards. At the Meadowlark junction, keep left on the main trail.

Dip across a shallow valley for 0.1 mile to a junction with Upper Dog Loop Trail. Go left on Sand Canyon Trail and descend northwest for 0.1 mile to the start of the Contemplative Trail. Keep right and follow Sand Canyon Trail north and then east back to the trailhead and parking lot.

Miles and Directions

0.0   Start at the trailhead at the west end of the main parking lot (GPS: 38.853554, -104.881362).

0.1   Reach the start of Sand Canyon Trail at the junction with a road. Go left.

0.25   At a junction, go right on Contemplative Trail (GPS: 38.851352, -104.884387).

0.8   Reach the end of Contemplative Trail and the junction with Sand Canyon Trail (GPS: 38.840697, -104.889396). Go left.

0.85   Go left at the junction with Quarry Pass Trail (GPS: 38.845333, -104.887611).

1.2   Reach the junction with Meadowlark Trail (GPS: 38.849772, -104.884780). Go straight.

1.3   Go left (west) at the junction with Upper Dog Loop Trail (GPS: 38.850357, -104.883668).

1.6   Arrive back at the trailhead and parking lot.

14 Coyote Gulch Trail and Creekbottom Loop

Wander through grassy meadows and lush creekside terrain while experiencing local flora and fauna at Bear Creek Nature Center.

Distance: 1.25-mile loop
Hiking time: About 1 hour
Difficulty: Easy; 140-foot elevation gain
Trail surface: Paved to gravel to dirt path
Best season: Year-round
Other trail users: Hikers only
Canine compatibility: No dogs allowed
Fees and permits: No fees or permits required
Maps: USGS Colorado Springs
Trail contacts: Bear Creek Nature Center, 245 Bear Creek Rd., Colorado Springs, CO 80906; (719) 520-6387; adm.elpasoco.com/Community Services/RecandCulturalSvc/ Pages/BearCreekNatureCenter .aspx
El Paso County Parks and Leisure Services, 2002 Creek Crossing, Colorado Springs, CO 80905, (719) 520-PLAY (7529), http://adm.elpasoco .com/CommunityServices/Park Operations/Pages/default.aspx

Finding the trailhead: From I-25 take the Cimarron Street/US 24 exit (exit 141). Drive west on US 24 for 2.1 miles to 26th Street. Turn left (south) on 26th Street and go 1.4 miles (past the switchbacks) to a stop sign at Gold Camp Road. Go straight through the intersection onto Bear Creek Road. Drive down a short hill and turn left (east) after 0.2 mile into the Bear Creek Nature Center parking lot. GPS: 38.828965, –104.879243

The Hike

This loop hike at the Bear Creek Nature Center, part of El Paso County's Bear Creek Park, links up trails that ring the outer perimeter of the park, offering tranquility on the western edge of Colorado Springs. The park, spreading across scrubby foothills below the mountains, is home to many bird species. You also have a good chance to see other wildlife, including mule deer, red foxes, ground squirrels, and garter snakes. Be sure to check out the nature center, which offers information about local ecosystems, dioramas, and interactive exhibits that are ideal for youngsters, as well as guided tours and interpretive programs (hours vary; check beforehand for availability).

Leave the plaza on the west side of the nature center on a paved trail that heads south. Walk about 100 feet, and go left (east) over a bridge that spans sandy-bottomed Bear Creek and pass the start of the Mountain Scrub Loop Trail and Songbird Trail. Continue straight ahead on the paved trail. Past the second Songbird Trail marker, the path becomes gravel. Interpretive signs and benches line the route. After passing the second turnoff to the right, take the next right turn after 0.2 mile and begin climbing south up the path. Helpful maps are located at nearly all trail junctions.

Hike uphill for 0.1 mile, passing a trail junction, to another trail junction at 0.3 mile. Turn left (southeast) and begin hiking on Coyote Gulch Trail, which offers good views east to Colorado Springs and the tawny prairie beyond.

The trail here skirts the eastern edge of an open, yucca-studded meadow, arcing toward the south and west before dropping into narrow Coyote Gulch. Continue through quiet

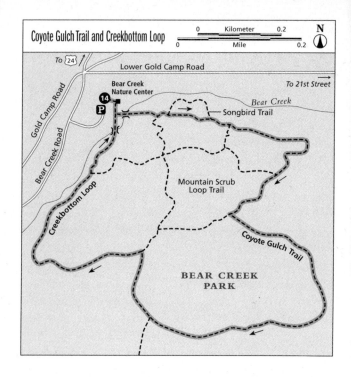

Coyote Gulch Trail and Creekbottom Loop

| 0 | Kilometer | 0.2 |
| 0 | Mile | 0.2 |

N

To 24

Lower Gold Camp Road

To 21st Street

Bear Creek
Nature Center

14

P

Bear Creek

Songbird Trail

Gold Camp Road

Bear Creek Road

Creekbottom Loop

Mountain Scrub
Loop Trail

Coyote Gulch Trail

**BEAR CREEK
PARK**

groves of scrub oak until you emerge from the gulch. Houses, separated by a narrow greenbelt, are to your left. Hike across a grassy plateau to a trail junction. Take the right trail and head back toward the north.

Descend an open meadow to a trail junction, turning left at the trail map by a large juniper onto Creekbottom Loop. The trail contours southwest above a wooded valley. Stairs lead down into the shady valley, growing ever greener as the sound of rushing water in Bear Creek intensifies. Follow the cool, shady trail alongside the creek through a lush riparian zone until you return to the main trailhead and parking lot.

Miles and Directions

0.0 Begin at the trailhead at the nature center (GPS: 38.829276, –104.878860).

0.05 Reach a trail junction (GPS: 38.829041, –104.878796). Go left over the bridge.

0.2 Arrive at the third trail junction on the right (GPS: 38.828799, –104.877099). Go right.

0.3 Reach a trail junction at the top of a hill (GPS: 38.828799, –104.877099). Go left on Coyote Gulch Trail.

0.8 Reach a trail junction in a meadow (GPS: 38.825713, –104.879051). Go right.

0.9 Reach a trail junction (GPS: 38.826898, –104.879057). Go left on Creekbottom Loop.

1.2 Reach the trail junction at the nature center. Go straight.

1.25 Arrive back at the trailhead.

15 Mount Cutler Trail

Climb through a pine and fir forest in North Cheyenne Cañon Park to the summit of 7,164-foot Mount Cutler, which offers panoramic views of Colorado Springs.

Distance: 1.9 miles out and back
Hiking time: 1 to 2 hours
Difficulty: Easy; 367-foot elevation gain
Trail surface: Singletrack dirt trail
Best season: Year-round; icy in winter
Other trail users: Runners
Canine compatibility: Leashed dogs permitted

Fees and permits: No fees or permits required
Maps: USGS Manitou Springs
Trail contacts: Colorado Springs Parks, Recreation, and Cultural Services, 1401 Recreation Way, Colorado Springs, CO 80905-1975; (719) 385-5940; https://coloradosprings .gov/department/76

Finding the trailhead: From I-25 take the Nevada Avenue/CO 115 exit (exit 140 B). Drive south on South Nevada Avenue/CO 115 for about a mile and turn right (west) onto Cheyenne Road. Follow Cheyenne Road for 2.6 miles to its end at Cheyenne Boulevard. (If you approach via Cheyenne Boulevard, stay right on Cheyenne Boulevard at this intersection.) Go left (west) on Cheyenne Boulevard for 0.1 mile to a Y intersection. Go right, through an open gate into North Cheyenne Cañon Park. Drive 1.4 miles up the park road to the Mount Cutler trailhead on the left. GPS: 38.791788, –104.887175

The Hike

Serene, peaceful, and seemingly remote, North Cheyenne Cañon tucks into the Front Range on the southwest side of

Colorado Springs. Just beyond charming residential districts, a winding road climbs west into this spectacular canyon, which is also one of the city's oldest parks.

The hike up Mount Cutler is the easiest and most accessible summit climb in the Pikes Peak region. Expect great views across North and South Cheyenne Cañons, an easy grade, peaceful pine and fir woods, and airy exposure on the last section. Be careful and watch your children as you hike along the exposed trail above South Cheyenne Cañon, especially if you make the short hike out to the east summit, which perches above dangerous and vertical cliffs. Some of the footing is on loose slippery gravel scattered atop the granite bedrock.

Mount Cutler offers stunning panoramic views from its rounded summit of dark forests spilling down steep mountainsides, the North and South Cheyenne Creek drainages, towering granite formations, and tumbling Seven Falls, as well as vistas of Colorado Springs and the high plains to the east. The wide trail climbs steadily but is an easy climb, with a thrilling touch of exposure as you traverse across the west- and south-facing shoulders of the mountain.

From the parking lot and trailhead at 6,797 feet in North Cheyenne Cañon, hike up the broad, well-used path through a dense evergreen forest that provides welcome shade in summer. The trail gently climbs and at 0.26 mile reaches an overlook with views of distant downtown Colorado Springs. The trail continues climbing, crossing steep slopes littered with fallen trees. The trail flattens out briefly beneath a squat rock tower and then bends through a gully and climbs again, reaching an outlook at 0.4 mile. An excellent view opens across the cliff-lined canyon to the sprawl of Colorado Springs.

At 0.5 mile is a saddle that separates North and South Cheyenne Cañons. The 1.3-mile Mount Muscoco Trail heads right here, climbing a good trail to its 8,020-foot summit. Keep straight ahead on the well-trod path for Mount Cutler. The trail traverses onto the dry southwest side of the mountain. Below, sparse pines cling to rocky soil. The narrow trail edges across an exposed slope, with steep cliffs and drop-offs to your right. Keep your children in check here. As you hike, look down to the right from the trail and you'll glimpse Seven Falls cascading far below.

The trail continues spiraling upward onto the south slope, passing a trail marker at a switchback at 0.75 mile. Keep left and scramble up the final steep trail section to 7,164-foot Mount Cutler's broad rounded summit at 0.95 mile. The summit offers 360° views, with the city and vast plains spreading east to the distant horizon and the monumental peaks of the Front Range looming to the west.

To return to the trailhead from Mount Cutler's summit, follow the trail back down. It's all downhill—and the views are just as good as on the way up.

Miles and Directions

0.0   Begin at the trailhead (GPS: 38.791788, -104.887175).

0.4   Arrive at an overlook.

0.5   Reach the saddle (GPS: 38.788101, -104.879245).

0.95 Arrive at the summit of Mount Cutler (GPS: 38.787864, -104.877840). Retrace your steps toward the trailhead.

1.9   Arrive back at the trailhead.

Option: To reach Mount Cutler's lower east summit, go left (east) from the main trail on one of two trails just below the

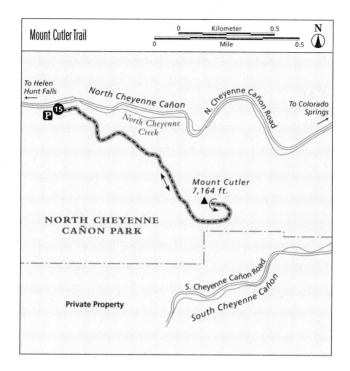

main summit. A short distance east of the main path, these two join together. Follow the trail another 0.25 mile east to Cutler's lower summit. This lofty perch, surrounded by airy cliffs, yields superb views of Colorado Springs and the Broadmoor Hotel area below.

16 Silver Cascade Falls Trail

This short hike begins at Helen Hunt Falls in upper North Cheyenne Cañon Park and climbs to a scenic viewpoint above Silver Cascade Falls, a rushing waterfall on a granite slab.

Distance: 0.7 mile out and back
Hiking time: 30 minutes to 1 hour
Difficulty: Easy; 200-foot elevation gain
Trail surface: Doubletrack dirt trail
Best season: Year-round; icy and snow packed in winter
Other trail users: Hikers only
Canine compatibility: Leashed dogs permitted

Fees and permits: No fees or permits required
Maps: USGS Manitou Springs
Trail contacts: Colorado Springs Parks, Recreation, and Cultural Services, 1401 Recreation Way, Colorado Springs, CO 80905-1975; (719) 385-5940; https://coloradosprings .gov/department/76

Finding the trailhead: From I-25 take exit 140 A or B for South Nevada Avenue. Drive south on South Nevada Avenue for 0.4 mile; turn right (west) onto West Cheyenne Road and drive 2.8 miles to the junction of North Cheyenne Cañon Road (right) and South Cheyenne Cañon Road (left). Turn right onto North Cheyenne Cañon Road and drive 2.6 miles to Helen Hunt Falls and a couple of large parking areas. The trailhead begins on the left side of the Helen Hunt Falls Visitor Center next to the falls. GPS: 38.788798, –104.902968

The Hike

The short, easy Silver Cascade Falls Trail begins at Helen Hunt Falls and climbs to an overlook perched above Silver

Cascade Falls, offering scenic views down North Cheyenne Cañon to Colorado Springs and the prairie beyond. Waterfalls are rarely found near Colorado Springs, despite the surrounding rugged mountains, and this trail offers two of the region's best falls. The hike is in North Cheyenne Cañon Park, a natural park administered by the city of Colorado Springs.

The dirt-and-gravel trail has easy grades and plenty of locations to stop and catch your breath at its 7,000-foot elevation. It can, however, be dangerous. In winter the first trail section past Helen Hunt Falls is usually icy and snow packed. Watch your footing so that you don't slip. The most dangerous part of the trail is the smooth granite slab that Silver Cascade Falls tumbles down. Do not venture onto the slab, or you might tumble down yourself. It's slippery, water polished, and steeper than it looks. The upper trail section is fenced for your safety. Keep an eye on your children, and don't let them wander onto the rock. Severe injuries and fatalities have occurred here.

Begin your hike at the Helen Hunt Falls Visitor Center, nicknamed the Cub, next to Helen Hunt Falls. The center, open daily in summer, offers lots of information as well as books about North Cheyenne Cañon and the Pikes Peak region.

From the trailhead on the left side of the visitor center, hike up stone steps to a bridge above 45-foot-high Helen Hunt Falls. This pretty waterfall, usually rushing with snowmelt in May and June, is named for famed nineteenth-century author and poet Helen Hunt Jackson, who often came here for inspiration and solace in the 1880s. After dying of cancer, she was buried in nearby South Cheyenne Cañon before being reinterred at Evergreen Cemetery in Colorado Springs.

After crossing the bridge, the trail bends west and slowly climbs along the southern edge of North Cheyenne Creek,

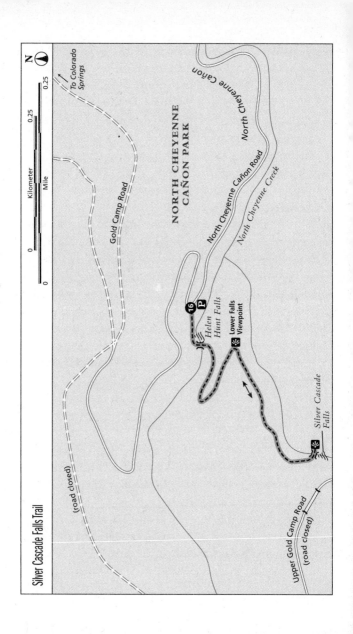

Silver Cascade Falls Trail

N

To Colorado
Springs

Gold Camp Road

(road closed)

Kilometer
0   0.25   0.25
Mile
0   0.25

North Cheyenne Cañon

North Cheyenne Cañon

NORTH CHEYENNE
CAÑON PARK

North Cheyenne Cañon Road

North Cheyenne Creek

16
P

Helen Hunt Falls

Lower Falls
Viewpoint

Silver Cascade
Falls

Upper Gold Camp Road
(road closed)

a dashing stream that originates to the west on Mount Almagre, the region's second-highest mountain. Doubling back left, the trail contours up across a forested slope to a lower viewpoint of Silver Cascade Falls at 0.2 mile. This is a good spot to grab a rest and enjoy the view.

The last trail segment heads south up the gravel trail. A convenient bench partway up allows for meditation, and a split-rail fence on the left keeps you and your children from straying onto the dangerous slick granite slab below. At 0.3 mile the trail levels out and crosses St. Mary's Creek on a small bridge. Beyond is a lookout point ringed with a stone wall above Silver Cascade Falls and the end of the trail.

Below the lookout, the creek dashes to white foam and spray as it cascades almost 200 feet down a broad water-polished slab. Again, don't venture beyond the stone wall. The slab below is treacherous, and the footing is polished and slippery. It's best to enjoy the view down North Cheyenne Cañon from above. To complete the hike, retrace your footsteps back down the trail to the parking lot.

Miles and Directions

0.0   Start at the trailhead next to Helen Hunt Falls (GPS: 38.788798, -104.902968).

0.1   The trail follows North Cheyenne Creek.

0.2   Reach the lower viewpoint of Silver Cascade Falls.

0.3   Cross a creek on a bridge.

0.35   Reach the upper viewpoint of Silver Cascade Falls (GPS: 38.787248, -104.905599). Retrace your steps.

0.7   Arrive back at the trailhead.

17 Gray Back Peak Trail

This pleasant singletrack trail with moderate grades ends with great views from the summit of 9,288-foot Gray Back Peak on the southern edge of the Pikes Peak massif.

Distance: 3.8 miles out and back

Hiking time: 2.5 to 3 hours

Difficulty: Moderate; 538-foot elevation gain

Trail surface: Singletrack dirt path

Best season: Mar through Nov; snow and ice in winter

Other trail users: Equestrians on the first part

Canine compatibility: Dogs permitted

Fees and permits: No fees or permits required

Maps: USGS Mount Big Chief

Trail contacts: Pike National Forest, Pikes Peak Ranger District, 601 South Weber St., Colorado Springs, CO 80903; (719) 636-1602; www.fs.usda.gov

Finding the trailhead: From I-25 take the Circle Drive exit (exit 138) and drive west on Circle Drive, which becomes Lake Avenue at its junction with CO 115. Continue west on Lake until it dead-ends at the Broadmoor Hotel. Turn right onto Lake Circle and drive 0.25 mile to a circular roundabout. Turn left at the roundabout onto Mesa Avenue and follow it around the west side of the Broadmoor Hotel and golf course. At a four-way intersection, go left onto El Pomar Road and follow it to an angling right turn onto Old Stage Road. (**Note:** Use caution driving on Old Stage Road; it's steep, often busy with traffic, and dusty, and can be muddy, icy, and slippery.) Follow the paved road until it becomes gravel at a sharp switchback. Continue up the twisting gravel road for about 6 miles to FR 371 at a sign for Emerald Valley Ranch. Turn left onto FR 371 and drive 0.3 mile on the narrow road to a saddle. Park on the left in a sloping parking area. GPS: 38.731464, −104.906657

The Hike

The 1.9-mile Gray Back Peak Trail offers a marvelous hike that climbs to the rocky summit of 9,288-foot Gray Back Peak, a high mountain on the southeast edge of the Pikes Peak massif. The summit yields great views of Emerald Valley to the west, Cheyenne Mountain to the northeast, and the brown plains below, stretching east toward Kansas. The gravel trail has generally moderate grades and is easy to follow. Horse strings from Emerald Valley Ranch often use the first half of the trail, so it is worn and eroded in places.

Begin from the parking area in the saddle at 8,750 feet. The trailhead is unmarked. Hike southeast on a narrow trail, slowly climbing up the western slope of a ridge. After 0.3 mile of steady uphill hiking, the trail passes a saddle and continues up the slope onto a broad ridge. At 0.7 mile you reach a 9,153-foot summit. It's a good spot to take a break and catch your breath. Check out the great views to the northwest of the abrupt cliffs on the east side of Mount Vigil.

Descend the loose gravel trail on the broad ridge to a saddle and then climb the ridge to a wooded knoll and drop down to a saddle at 1.3 miles. Take note of the trail junction at this saddle. A horse path continues up left, while the Gray Back Peak Trail goes sharply right (south). A cairn, or stack of rocks, usually marks this junction. The next trail section, from here to the summit, offers excellent hiking through quiet woods on a good narrow trail.

Hike south on west-facing slopes with open views across Emerald Valley, and at 1.6 miles you reach a high saddle between Gray Back Peak to the right and an unnamed 9,410-foot summit to the left. Dense aspens interspersed with fir and spruce blanket the saddle. As you continue

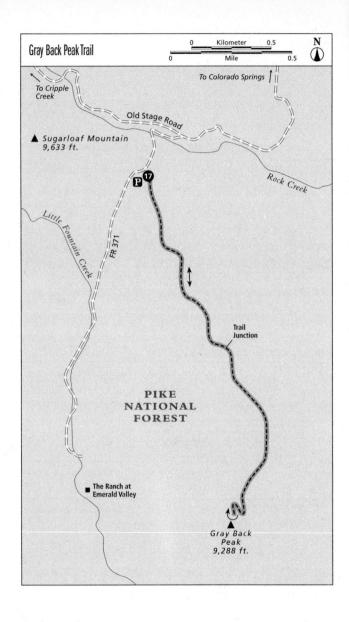

Gray Back Peak Trail

Kilometer
0   0.5

Mile
0   0.5

N

To Cripple Creek

To Colorado Springs

Old Stage Road

▲ Sugarloaf Mountain
9,633 ft.

Rock Creek

P 17

Little Fountain Creek

FR 371

Trail Junction

PIKE
NATIONAL
FOREST

■ The Ranch at
Emerald Valley

▲ Gray Back Peak
9,288 ft.

hiking south from the saddle, the trail rises and begins switchbacking up the peak's steep east flank. After 1.9 miles of hiking, you finally emerge onto the 9,288-foot-high summit of Gray Back Peak.

Relax in the shade of twisted trees on the summit and enjoy the views. Below are sharp, remote canyons on the southern edge of the Front Range, and in the distance to the south rise the dark bulk of the Wet Mountains and the distant twin Spanish Peaks.

To return, follow the trail back down to the saddle and then north to the trail junction. Remember to go left. You'll have a couple hills to climb on your way back to the parking area.

Miles and Directions

0.0 Start at the unmarked trailhead (GPS: 38.731464, -104.906657).

0.7 Reach the summit of a hill.

1.1 Reach the second summit, with views of Gray Back Peak to the south.

1.3 Come to a saddle and trail junction. Keep right on the main trail.

1.6 Reach the saddle between Gray Back Peak and an unnamed peak.

1.9 Arrive at the summit of Gray Back Peak (GPS: 38.7114, -104.8999). Retrace your steps, remembering to turn left at the trail junction.

3.8 Arrive back at the trailhead.

18 Coyote Run Trail

This fun hike in Cheyenne Mountain State Park explores the hills above the park visitor center, passing open meadows, scrub oak forests, and scattered ponderosa pines.

Distance: 1.4-mile lollipop
Hiking time: 1 to 2 hours
Difficulty: Easy; 130-foot elevation gain
Trail surface: Singletrack dirt path
Best season: Year-round
Other trail users: Mountain bikers
Canine compatibility: No dogs allowed

Fees and permits: Daily fee to enter the park
Maps: USGS Cheyenne Mountain; trail map available at park website
Trail contacts: Cheyenne Mountain State Park, 410 JL Ranch Heights Rd., Colorado Springs, CO 80926; (719) 576-2016; http://cpw.state.co.us/placestogo /Parks/cheyennemountain

Finding the trailhead: From I-25 take the South Academy Boulevard exit (exit 135) and drive west on South Academy past Pikes Peak Community College. Continue west and turn south onto CO 115. Drive south on the divided highway to a stoplight. The park entrance is to your right, opposite Fort Carson Gate 1. Drive west on JL Ranch Heights Road to the park visitor center and entrance station. Park in the visitor center lot and pay your entrance fee at the visitor center. The trailhead is on the west side of the parking lot at a kiosk. GPS: 38.734981, −104.819768

The Hike

The Coyote Run Trail is a great hike for kids and families in the hills above the Cheyenne Mountain State Park Visitor

Center, which makes a good stop with its informative displays as well as books about the area's natural history. The easy-to-follow singletrack trail has minimal elevation gain, gradual grades, and plenty of rest stops. It's well marked with signposts at regular intervals.

Start the hike on the west side of the visitor center parking lot at 6,055 feet. The trailhead is between two benches right of a ramada with a display about trail etiquette. Hike west 100 feet to a sign on the left that explains the web of life. Continue to a registration box on the right, and sign in.

The trail heads west alongside a dry wash and through scrub oak thickets for 0.12 mile to a Y junction with a trail sign in a garden of granite boulders. This point is the start of the Coyote Run loop trail. Go left (south) to begin the loop.

The next 0.8-mile trail segment runs south, crossing the park road, to a junction with Boulder Run Trail. The trail twists through shallow wooded draws studded with boulders and shaded by oaks and pines. Several signs about park wildlife, including black bears, prairie dogs, and mountain lions, are scattered along the way. The trail reaches the road at its turnoff to the Limekiln Grove trailhead. Cross the road and pick up the trail on the road's west side.

Pass some boulders and then swing across meadows on the northern edge of broad Limekiln Valley to a trail fork with a granite block. The left fork is 1.03-mile Zook Loop Trail, another pleasant hike. Take the right fork and stay on Coyote Run Trail. The trail bends north and gradually climbs to a Y junction with Boulder Run Trail, which heads left.

Go right on Coyote Run Trail, and hike past picnic tables to a building and a road. Following small signs with arrows pointing the way, walk along the right (east) side of the building on a sidewalk; cross the road at a crosswalk to the

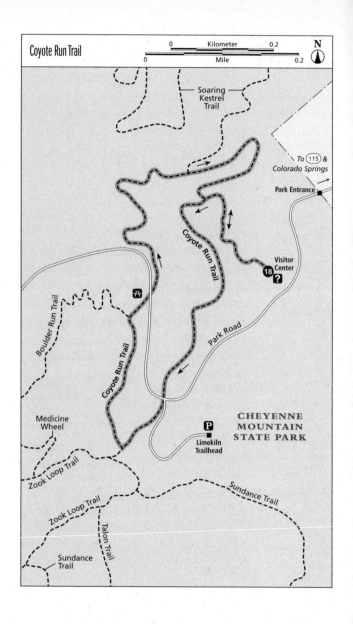

Coyote Run Trail

Kilometer
0   0.2
0   Mile   0.2

N

Soaring
Kestrel
Trail

To 115 &
Colorado Springs

Park Entrance

Coyote Run Trail

Visitor
Center
18
?

Park Road

Boulder Run Trail

Coyote Run Trail

Medicine
Wheel

P
Limekiln
Trailhead

CHEYENNE
MOUNTAIN
STATE PARK

Zook Loop Trail

Zook Loop Trail

Sundance Trail

Talon Trail

Sundance
Trail

east side of the road and another building and small parking area for the picnic area. Cross the road to the left (north) and pick up Coyote Run Trail.

Hike north on the trail, dipping in and out of shallow, rocky drainages; after 1.1 miles reach a junction with Soaring Kestrel Trail past a bench and a ponderosa pine. Keep right on Coyote Run Trail.

The next trail section descends 0.12 mile from the junction to the lower trail fork near the visitor center. The trail bends sharply right (south) and descends open terrain, passing a sign about rattlesnakes. Prairie rattlers do live in the park but are rarely seen. These warm, rocky slopes form an ideal habitat for rattlesnakes. It's more likely, however, that you will see a bull snake, which resembles and mimics a rattlesnake. Continue your descent past small pines to the first trail junction at a shaded rock garden. Go left (east) and hike 0.1 mile back to the trailhead and visitor center.

Miles and Directions

0.0 Start at the trailhead at the visitor center parking lot (GPS: 38.734981, -104.819768).

0.12 Reach the trail junction at the start of the loop trail (GPS: 38.736009, -104.820484). Go left.

0.9 Go right at the junction with Boulder Run Trail (GPS: 38.734155, -104.823598).

1.0 Reach a picnic area and roads.

1.1 Keep right at the junction with Soaring Kestrel Trail (GPS: 38.737017, -104.82027).

1.3 Reach the trail junction at the end of the loop trail. Go left.

1.4 Arrive back at the trailhead and parking area.

19 Blackmer Loop Trail

This secluded hike traverses grassy meadows, scrub oak thickets, and ponderosa pine woods in the western sector of Cheyenne Mountain State Park.

Distance: 4.7-mile lollipop
Hiking time: 2 to 3 hours
Difficulty: Moderate; 250-foot elevation gain
Trail surface: Singletrack dirt path
Best season: Year-round; possibly icy in winter
Other trail users: Mountain bikers
Canine compatibility: No dogs allowed

Fees and permits: Daily fee to enter the park
Maps: USGS Cheyenne Mountain; trail map available at park website
Trail contacts: Cheyenne Mountain State Park, 410 JL Ranch Heights Rd., Colorado Springs, CO 80926; (719) 576-2016; http://cpw.state .co.us/placestogo/Parks /cheyennemountain

Finding the trailhead: From I-25 take the South Academy Boulevard exit (exit 135) and drive west on South Academy past Pikes Peak Community College. Continue west for a couple of miles and turn south onto CO 115. Drive south on the divided highway to a stoplight. The park entrance is to your right, opposite Fort Carson Gate 1. Drive west on JL Ranch Heights Road to the park visitor center and entrance station. After paying your entrance fee, drive up the park road to the campground. Park on the right in a large lot at the camper services building. The trailhead for the first leg—Raccoon Ridge Trail—is at the north side of the parking lot. GPS: 38.73769, –104.828351

The Hike

The 3.5-mile-long Blackmer Loop Trail, threading through shallow ravines and contouring across gentle hillsides, is one of the best easy day hikes not only in the 1,680-acre Cheyenne Mountain State Park but also in the entire Colorado Springs area. The singletrack path, shared with mountain bikers, offers great hiking as well as lots of solitude, interesting plant communities, plenty of wildlife, and great views of Cheyenne Mountain towering above. The trail is well marked with seventeen round trail markers. Other markers evenly spaced along the trail give GPS coordinates in case you get lost or want to track the trail. Hiking the trail requires parking at the camper services building and following Raccoon Ridge Trail and part of Boulder Run Trail to reach the start of Blackmer Loop, making the entire hike 4.7 miles long.

To begin the hike, drive up the park road from the visitor center and park at a large lot on the right side of the road at the campground visitor services area. From here you have two choices to reach the Blackmer trailhead. The scenic alternative is to follow the 0.5-mile Raccoon Ridge Trail, which begins at the north side of the parking lot and spirals southwest past some tent campsites to the park road and its junction with Boulder Run Trail. Hiking this trail adds another mile to your round-trip hike.

Alternatively, park at the lot and hike 0.3 mile down the road to the same trail junction on the right. Look for the Boulder Run Trail and a marker on the right (west) side of the road and to the right of a concrete drain and locked gate.

The first trail segment follows Boulder Run Trail for 0.1 mile to the start of the Blackmer Loop Trail. Hike west through scrub oak groves and broad meadows to a Y junction at 6,408 feet on a south-facing hill. Both forks are for Blackmer Loop. Take the right fork. A park trail map is located on the right side of the junction.

Hike west on the trail for 0.36 mile toward a junction with Cougar's Shadow Trail. The trail slowly climbs as it swings through meadows flanked by scrub oak. Stop at a bench with a view to the east and read an interpretive sign that details the area's earliest inhabitants, including the Ute Indians. Past the bench, the trail works southwest through meadows. Keep an eye out for bull snakes in the grass by the trail's edge.

Past some boulders, the trail turns south and reaches the junction with Cougar's Shadow Trail below shady pines. Go straight (left) on the main trail. Cougar's Shadow Trail, a 0.85-mile path, is an alternative to Blackmer here. It climbs southwest and then contours south and drops down to meet Blackmer farther south.

The next trail section runs southwest for 0.88 mile to the southern Cougar's Shadow Trail junction. This part offers great hiking, with the trail threading through boulder gardens, passing beneath ponderosa pines, and edging grassy glades rimmed with scrub oak as the trail climbs to its high point. To the west rises 9,565-foot Cheyenne Mountain. Several signs about bats, climate, and ponderosa pines are located along the way. At the ponderosa sign is a bench. Take a seat here to admire a hardy ponderosa pine growing from a crack in a 10-foot-high granite boulder.

Past the high point, the trail dips down and meets Cougar's Shadow Trail in a wooded ravine. Go left (east) at this three-way junction. The next Blackmer Loop Trail segment runs northeast for 1.41 miles, twisting down wooded slopes and following shallow draws filled with boulders. Occasional breaks in the trees allow views eastward to Fort Carson and the prairie. As the trail descends, the forest thins, with scrub oak and meadows becoming prevalent. At the edge of a shallow valley, Blackmer reaches a three-way junction. A side trail heads right to join the Zook Loop and Medicine Wheel Trails. Stay left on the main trail. There's a trail map at the junction.

The last section of Blackmer Loop climbs 0.75 mile from the junction back to the beginning of the loop and the end of Boulder Run Trail. The trail steadily climbs uphill, passing through jumbles of granite boulders in the valley before reaching open meadows on a south-facing slope. An interpretive sign details the transition life zone that you're passing through—a species-rich ecosystem where the foothills scrubland meets the montane forest. Past the sign, the trail edges across the hillside and meets the three-way junction that marks the start of the Blackmer Loop.

Go straight (east) on the main trail, which now becomes Boulder Run Trail. Hike 0.1 mile back to the park road; then cross the road and follow Raccoon Ridge Trail for 0.55 mile back to the parking lot.

Miles and Directions

0.0   Start on Raccoon Ridge Trail, located at the north side of the camper services building parking lot (GPS: 38.73769, -104.828351).

0.5   Reach a junction with Raccoon Ridge Trail and the park road (GPS: 38.734753, -104.830736). Cross the road to access Boulder Run Trail.

0.6   A Y junction marks the start of Blackmer Loop Trail (GPS: 38.735111, -104.832847). Go right.

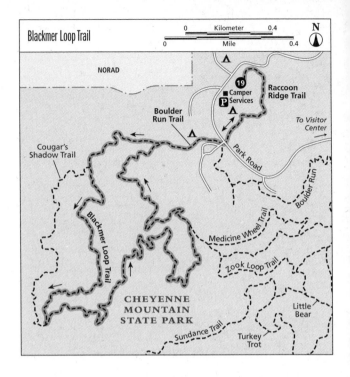

Blackmer Loop Trail

0.9 Go left (straight) at the three-way junction with the north end of Cougar's Shadow Trail.

1.8 Go left at the three-way junction with the south end of Cougar's Shadow Trail.

3.2 Keep straight (left) at the three-way junction with the side trail to Zook Loop and Medicine Wheel Trails (GPS: 38.731573, –104.831489).

4.1 Return to the Y junction with Boulder Run Trail. Go straight.

4.2 Reach the park road and cross it to the start of Raccoon Ridge Trail. Go straight.

4.7 Arrive back at the parking lot and camper services building.

20 Manitou Lake Trail

Manitou Lake Trail is an easy, mile-long trail that encircles Manitou Lake north of Woodland Park and Pikes Peak. It's an ideal hike for families and children with easy grades, nature study, and scenic views.

Distance: 1-mile loop
Hiking time: About 1 hour
Difficulty: Easy; minimal elevation gain
Trail surface: Dirt path
Best season: Mar through Nov; summer is best
Other trail users: None
Canine compatibility: Leashed dogs permitted

Fees and permits: Day entrance fee required
Schedule: Open year-round
Maps: USGS Mount Deception
Trail contacts: Pike National Forest, Pikes Peak Ranger District, 601 South Weber St., Colorado Springs, CO 80903; (719) 636-1602; www.fs.usda.gov

Finding the trailhead: From Colorado Springs and I-25, drive west on US 24 to Woodland Park. Turn north on the west side of Woodland Park on CO 67 and drive 7.8 miles to Manitou Lake Recreation Area. Turn right (east) into the area and park in the first or second parking lot and the trailhead. GPS: 39.089956, -105.098477.

A day-use entrance fee is required. Allow 45 minutes to drive from Colorado Springs to the trailhead.

The Hike

Manitou Lake Picnic Area, administered by Pike National Forest, is a small parkland north of Woodland Park. The easy, mile-long Manitou Lake Trail #670, strolling around the perimeter of the scenic 5-acre Manitou Lake, offers superb views of snowcapped Pikes Peak to the south, good bird-watching with a variety of songbirds and waterfowl, and fishing in the trout-stocked lake. Hand-paddled craft like canoes are allowed on the lake, but swimming and motor boats are not permitted.

The trail, a good introduction to hiking for kids, is partly accessible for strollers and wheelchairs, although it may be impassable when it's wet or muddy.

Begin the hike at a trailhead just west of Manitou Lake's north end. Cross a bridge over the dam's spillway, where you can stop and watch the rushing water cascade down a chute on the dam. On the east side of the bridge, continue hiking straight ahead atop the earthen dam.

The trail forks at the east end of the dam at 0.1 mile. Take the left fork and hike up and around a knoll. The right fork, which is usually wet in spring and early summer, stays beside the lake and offers access for fishermen.

The trail passes through a ponderosa pine and Douglas fir forest and then crosses a lush meadow before gently descending to the willow-lined lake. You'll reach a trail fork at 0.5 mile. Go straight on the main trail, heading southwest along the lake. Pass a bench before a marshland at the south end of Manitou Lake.

The trail next crosses an elevated boardwalk above the marsh. Thick stands of cattails border the trail, making a perfect refuge for birds. Watch for red-winged blackbirds and kingfishers perched on the cattails. An interpretive sign describes the functions of a wetland. The trail continues, crossing Trout Creek's braided inlet stream, to another interpretive sign at 0.7 mile. The boardwalk ends past the third interpretive display, and the trail climbs gently along the lake's west shore to a picnic area with tables and fire grates.

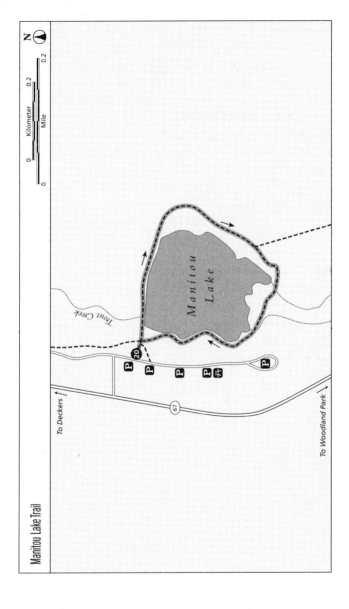

Manitou Lake Trail

Continue hiking north under shady ponderosa pines to the bridge, trailhead, and parking lots.

To lengthen the hike, go left or south at the trail fork just before you enter the marsh and hike across a meadow. This path runs beside the fenced boundary of Colorado Campground to CO 67. Cross the highway and turn right or north. Head back to the lake on asphalt Trail #699, a 4.2-mile-long bike trail that connects Manitou Lake Picnic Area with two campgrounds to the south.

Miles and Directions

0.0 Start at the trailhead on the east side of the entrance road (GPS: 39.089956, –105.098477).

0.1 Walk across the top of the earthen dam.

0.5 Reach a trail fork. Go straight (GPS: 39.087200, –105.095405).

0.7 Cross a boardwalk through a marsh at the south end of the lake.

1.0 Arrive back at the trailhead.

21 Outlook Ridge and Lost Pond Loop

This popular hike down Outlook Ridge in Mueller State Park offers three scenic overlooks and then a return hike up a wooded valley past Lost Pond.

Distance: 4.65-mile loop

Hiking time: 1 to 2 hours

Difficulty: Moderate; 400-foot elevation loss and gain

Trail surface: Single- and doubletrack dirt path

Best season: Year-round; can be icy in winter

Other trail users: Mountain bikers

Canine compatibility: No dogs allowed

Fees and permits: Daily fee to enter the park

Maps: USGS Divide; trail map available at park website

Trail contacts: Mueller State Park, PO Box 39, 21045 Hwy. 67 South, Divide, CO 80814; (719) 687-2366; http://cpw.state.co.us/placestogo/Parks/Mueller

Finding the trailhead: Take the Cimarron Street/US 24 exit (exit 141) from I-25. Drive west on US 24 up Ute Pass and through Woodland Park. Continue west on US 24 to the town of Divide. Turn left (south) on CO 67 toward Cripple Creek. Drive 3.8 miles to the park entrance and turn right (west) into the park. After paying the entrance fee, follow Wapiti Road for 1.5 miles to the Outlook Ridge parking area and trailhead on the left (south) side of the road. Restrooms, picnic tables, and water are available at the trailhead. GPS: 38.881137, –105.181298

The Hike

The Outlook Ridge and Lost Pond Loop hike combines seven trails into a single hike. The trail mileage can be shortened, depending on whether you hike out to the three overlooks along the way. Each of those out-and-back trails is 0.6 mile. The four main trails the hike follows are the Outlook Ridge Trail (Trail 7), Geer Pond Trail (Trail 25), Lost Pond Trail (Trail 11), and Revenuer's Ridge (Trail 1). The easy-to-follow route is well marked by posts with trail numbers and blue arrows.

The loop hike, following a ridge with three overlooks and returning up a wooded valley, divides into two sections. The first section, along a ridge, offers picture-perfect views of Pikes Peak to the southeast. The second segment threads up a short, steep valley filled with conifers and aspens and filled with birdsong and wildflowers in summer.

Mueller State Park spreads across 5,112 acres with an average elevation of 9,600 feet on the west side of 14,115-foot Pikes Peak. The park offers 55 miles of hiking on thirty-seven trails that explore its valleys, ridges, and mountains. Many trails lead to scenic overlooks with far-ranging views of the Sangre de Cristo and Sawatch Ranges. Mueller has 132 campsites and is renowned as the best wildlife watching area in the Pikes Peak region, with lots of mammals including black bear, elk, and mule deer. The park's sheer size and lack of roads ensure seclusion and isolation.

The park's web of trails can be linked together to form loop hikes of varying lengths and difficulty. Trails range from short and easy to long and challenging. Pick up the trail map when you enter the park or download a copy from the park's website to plan other adventures.

The hike begins at the Outlook Ridge trailhead at 9,680 feet on the west side of Wapiti Road past the park visitor center. Picnic tables, restrooms, and water are available. Sign the register at the trailhead kiosk. The smooth doubletrack trail, an old road, heads west down Outlook Ridge and after 0.1 mile reaches a junction with Revenuer's Ridge Trail (Trail 1), the return trail for the last leg of the hike. Go straight.

The trail dips and rolls, with occasional views south into Hay Creek Valley, and after 0.5 mile reaches a junction with Raven Ridge Overlook Trail (Trail 8) on a slight uphill. Go left (south) on Trail 8 for great views. Raven Ridge Trail traverses a meadow and then drops for 0.3 mile to a spectacular overlook of granite benches. Watch children here, since the overlook is unfenced. This is the best overlook on the hike, with Pikes Peak looming to the east. After enjoying the view, return 0.3 mile uphill to Outlook Ridge Trail and turn left.

Hike down the broad ridge through aspens and conifers. After another 0.3 mile is a junction with Red Tail Overlook Trail (Trail 9) on a bend. Go left (south) on Red Tail and hike 0.3 mile downhill to a timber staircase and end at another spectacular overlook. This point, lower than Raven Ridge Overlook, is a smooth slab perched above cliffs and Brook Pond. Retrace your steps uphill to Outlook Ridge Trail and go left.

The trail descends steeply for 0.3 mile and reaches the junction with the Long Eagle Overlook Trail (Trail 10), the third overlook, at a bench. Go left on Long Eagle, climbing a short hill and then following a level ridge to a viewpoint at 0.3 mile. Return to the junction with Outlook Ridge Trail and go left (northeast).

Follow the doubletrack trail for 100 feet to a junction on the left with a sign: "Trail 7 Bypass to Avoid Steep Hills." Go left on the bypass, avoiding a steep hill and descent on the other side by contouring northeast. Follow the singletrack trail through dense spruce and fir forest for 0.2 mile to a junction with the steep alternative Trail 7. Continue straight for 0.1 mile across a trickling creek to a major trail junction with Geer Pond Trail (Trail 25) and the end of Outlook Ridge Trail (Trail 7). Go right on Trail 25.

The next trail segment follows Geer Pond Trail for 0.4 mile; then Geer Pond Trail becomes Lost Pond Trail (Trail 11). The segment initially climbs a steep hill on the doubletrack trail out of the drainage. From the top of the ascent, traverse above the shady valley. The roadbed narrows in a swampy area with dense forest, and the hike reaches Lost Pond after 3.65 miles. The small pond is tucked into a pastoral pocket of forest and meadow.

Leave the pond by climbing north on the wide trail, now Lost Pond Trail (Trail 11), to the head of a valley. Bend right and continue climbing east to a trail junction 0.3 mile from Lost Pond. Continue climbing another 0.1 mile to the Lost Pond trailhead and parking area. Below the parking area is a junction with Revenuer's Ridge Trail (Trail 1). Go right (south) on Trail 1.

The last hike section travels 0.5 mile south along Revenuer's Ridge Trail, dipping through vales and crossing wooded slopes until it intersects Outlook Ridge Trail (Trail 7). Go left on Trail 7 for 0.1 mile to the Outlook Ridge trailhead and parking area.

Miles and Directions

0.0   Start at the Outlook Ridge parking area, trailhead, and picnic area (GPS: 38.881137, -105.181298).

0.1   Go straight at the junction with Revenuer's Ridge Trail (Trail 1) on the right.

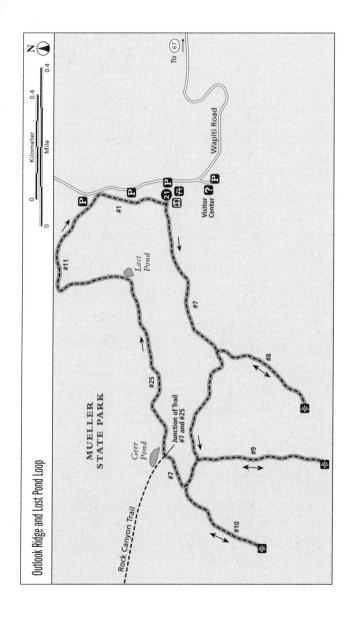

Outlook Ridge and Lost Pond Loop

MUELLER STATE PARK

Rock Canyon Trail

Geer Pond

Lost Pond

Junction of Trail #7 and #25

Visitor Center

Wapiti Road

To 67

#1
#7
#8
#9
#10
#11
#25

N

Kilometer
Mile
0   0.4

0.5 Reach the junction with Raven Ridge Overlook Trail (Trail 8) (GPS: 38.879316, –105.188835). Go left on Trail 8 to the overlook. Return to Outlook Ridge Trail (Trail 7) and go left (west).

1.4 Reach the junction with Red Tail Overlook Trail (Trail 9) (GPS: 38.879859, –105.193309). Go left for 0.3 mile on Trail 9 to an overlook. Return to Outlook Ridge Trail (Trail 7) and go left (west).

2.3 Reach the junction with Lone Eagle Overlook Trail (Trail 10) (GPS: 38.880496, –105.194939). Go left for 0.3 mile on Trail 10 to an overlook. Return to Outlook Ridge Trail (Trail 7) and go left (northeast).

2.95 Go left at the junction with the Trail 7 bypass.

3.25 Trail 7 ends at the junction with Geer Pond Trail (Trail 25) (GPS: 38.88116, –105.191887). Go right on Trail 25.

3.65 Trail 25 ends at Lost Pond. Continue straight on Lost Pond Trail (Trail 11).

4.05 Reach the Lost Pond trailhead and the junction with Revenuer's Ridge Trail (Trail 1) (GPS: 38.882698, –105.181915). Go right on Trail 1.

4.55 Reach the junction with Outlook Ridge Trail (Trail 7). Go left on Trail 7 for 0.1 mile to the trailhead.

4.65 Arrive back at the trailhead.

22 Grouse Mountain Overlook Trail

This fun hike climbs to the 9,843-foot summit of Grouse Mountain and a spectacular overlook that offers scenic views of Pikes Peak and Mueller State Park.

Distance: 0.8 mile out and back

Hiking time: 30 minutes to 1 hour

Difficulty: Moderate; 200-foot elevation gain

Trail surface: Single- and doubletrack dirt path

Best season: Year-round; can be icy and snowy in winter

Other trail users: First trail section open to mountain bikers and equestrians

Canine compatibility: No dogs allowed

Fees and permits: Daily fee to enter the park

Schedule: Trail closed from June 1 to 20 for elk calving

Maps: USGS Divide; trail map available at park website

Trail contacts: Mueller State Park, PO Box 39, 21045 Hwy. 67 South, Divide, CO 80814; (719) 687-2366; http://cpw.state .co.us/placestogo/Parks/Mueller

Finding the trailhead: Take the Cimarron Street/US 24 exit (exit 141) from I-25. Drive west on US 24 up Ute Pass and through Woodland Park. Continue west on US 24 to the town of Divide. Turn left (south) onto CO 67 toward Cripple Creek. Drive 3.8 miles to the park entrance and turn right (west) into the park. After paying the entrance fee, follow Wapiti Road past the visitor center and through the campground to the Grouse Mountain trailhead at the end of the road. Park in a large lot and begin at the trailhead at the north end of the lot. There are restrooms at the parking area. GPS: 38.902393, -105.183241

The Hike

The Grouse Mountain Overlook Trail (Trail 16) climbs to the rocky summit of 9,843-foot Grouse Mountain, the highest point in Mueller State Park. It offers relatively easy hiking with a gradual grade and a rocky summit with views of Pikes Peak, the park's shaggy hills and valleys, and distant vistas of snow-covered mountains. This is a great hike for families and kids, who will enjoy climbing a peak. The wide trail is easy to follow and designated with trail markers at every intersection. The trail is closed from June 1 to 20 every year for elk calving.

Begin at the Grouse Mountain trailhead at the northern end of the park road and campground. A wooden kiosk at the trailhead has a map, park rules, and information about black bears, which are common in the park. The hike, beginning on the Cheesman Ranch Trail (Trail 17), passes through a gate to an interpretive sign that explains the park's different habitats and the animals found in them.

Hike north 100 feet on the smooth doubletrack trail to a junction. Go straight on Trail 17. The left trail is the Homestead Trail (Trail 12), which heads west into a valley. The Grouse Mountain Overlook Trail gently climbs through a mixed conifer and aspen forest interspersed with open meadows. At 0.1 mile is a sign detailing turkey and blue grouse, commonly found in this habitat.

Farther along, Trail 17 bends to the right and at 0.2 mile reaches a junction with Grouse Mountain Overlook Trail (Trail 16). Go left on Trail 16. A trail marker with a white arrow points the way. The trail from here to the summit is for hikers only; no mountain bikes or horses are allowed.

The doubletrack trail swings west and begins climbing through a spruce and fir forest floored with mountain juniper. Glades of quaking aspen and meadows spill down the east side of the mountain. After a short ascent you reach the humped summit of Grouse Mountain. There is a good view on the east side of the summit of the northeast flank of Pikes Peak, with dark evergreen forests ending at timberline. The granite cliffs at The Crags, on Pikes Peak's north flank, can also be seen.

For the best views, though, you need to continue hiking south from the summit to a rocky lower point. This singletrack trail threads along a ridge, descending through boulder gardens to a twisted dead tree and an outcrop of granite boulders. Watch your children here—the overlook is unfenced.

Sit down on a boulder, crack open an energy bar, have a gulp of water, and enjoy the spacious view. To the east tower Pikes Peak and conical Sentinel Point. To the south rises pyramid-shaped Mount Pisgah above the old mining town of Cripple Creek. The sawtooth line of peaks to the southwest is the Sangre de Cristo Range, with nine of Colorado's 14,000-foot peaks and a lot of wild country. To the west spread the wooded valleys and hills of Mueller State Park; beyond them, poking against the western horizon, is the Sawatch Range. After resting, pick yourself up and return 0.4 mile along the same trails to the trailhead.

Miles and Directions

0.0   Start at the Grouse Mountain trailhead at the end of the park road (GPS: 38.902393, -105.183241). After 100 feet come to a trail junction. Go straight on Trail 17.

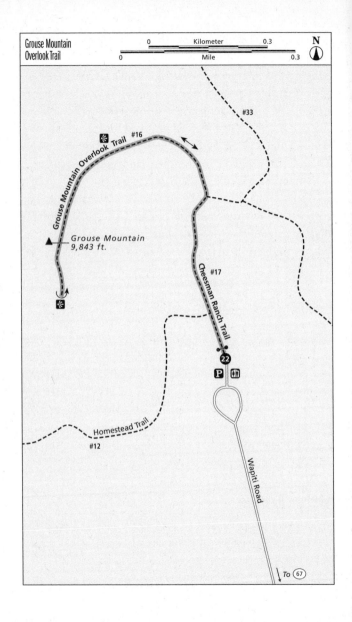

0   Kilometer   0.3

0   Mile   0.3

N

#33

Grouse Mountain Overlook Trail   #16

Grouse Mountain
9,843 ft.

Cheesman Ranch Trail   #17

22

P

Homestead Trail

#12

Wapiti Road

To 67

0.2 Go left at the trail junction onto Grouse Mountain Overlook Trail (Trail 16).

0.35 Reach the summit of Grouse Mountain (GPS: 38.903799, –105.186014).

0.4 Reach the overlook on the south side of the Grouse Mountain summit. Retrace your steps.

0.8 Arrive back at the trailhead and parking area.

23 The Crags Trail

After a short climb, this excellent hike leads through serene meadows below granite cliffs and boulder-strewn hillsides, with excellent views of Pikes Peak's northern shoulders.

Distance: 4 miles out and back
Hiking time: 2 to 3 hours
Difficulty: Easy; 700-foot elevation gain
Trail surface: Singletrack dirt trail
Best season: Apr through Oct; snowy in winter
Other trail users: Mountain bikers
Canine compatibility: Leashed dogs permitted

Fees and permits: No fees or permits required
Maps: USGS Pikes Peak and Woodland Park
Trail contacts: Pike National Forest, Pikes Peak Ranger District, 601 South Weber St., Colorado Springs, CO 80903; (719) 636-1602; www.fs.usda.gov
Other: Skis or snowshoes required in winter

Finding the trailhead: Take the Cimarron Street/US 24 exit (exit 141) from I-25. Follow US 24 west for about 24 miles up Ute Pass and through Woodland Park to the town of Divide. Turn left (south) onto CO 67 and drive 4.3 miles south to a left (east) turn onto Teller CR 62, marked with a "Crags Campground" sign. Follow the rough dirt road through the Rocky Mountain Mennonite Camp for 3.2 miles to a parking lot on the right surrounded by a split-rail fence. The trailhead is across the road, next to the restrooms. The Crags Campground is up the road about 0.2 mile. Alternatively, hike up the road through the campground to The Crags trailhead at its east end. GPS: 38.873772, -105.123712

The Hike

With gentle grades and unsurpassed mountain beauty, The Crags Trail (FS Trail 664) may be the perfect summer day hike in the Pikes Peak region. The trail slowly climbs up a subalpine valley below high summits, offering exposure and mountain views, but your thighs and lungs won't feel the burn like they would if you climbed the Devil's Playground Trail from here to the summit of 14,115-foot Pikes Peak. The trail winds up a beautiful wide valley, with wildflower-strewn meadows along Fourmile Creek, warm summer temperatures, and plentiful wildlife, including elk.

Take your time on this hike. Although the trail is relatively easy, its starting elevation is 10,040 feet and it ends at 10,800 feet. If you come from sea level, watch for altitude sickness, including headache and nausea. On summer afternoons, stay alert for severe thunderstorms with lightning moving across The Crags. Carry a raincoat and retreat to your car if you see incoming bad weather. Drinking water is available at The Crags Campground near the trailhead.

From the trailhead by the restrooms, the trail crosses Fourmile Creek, and the most difficult part of the hike begins. The trail switchbacks up a steep hillside, quickly gaining elevation before leveling off above The Crags Campground. Curve around a hillside and drop back down to a trail junction at the creek. Stay to the left, minding the trail marker for The Crags and paralleling the tumbling creek.

The trail passes through jumbled granite boulders before opening into a broad, grassy expanse. The trail heads east up the narrowing valley before reaching a larger meadow. The creek makes wide meanders across the valley floor, its banks densely lined with willows. Outcroppings of granite cliffs line the hillside to the left. Aspen trees and tall Englemann spruce and subalpine fir trees stand sentinel-like along the edge of the meadow. Ahead rises Pangborn's Pinnacle, a mighty granite dome that towers above the valley.

The Crags Trail briefly jogs to the left, climbing higher before dropping back into the meadow. Approaching a large granite dome on the north, the trail splits. Keep to the right track, with a cliff to the left. The trail then tracks through a swampy marshland before climbing back onto solid ground.

The bare northwest shoulder of Pikes Peak looms to the right, and other cliffs and crags fill steep slopes above the narrowing valley. When the valley crimps down, the trail passes a cliff with a shelter cave at its base to the right at 1.2 miles. This is an excellent place to rest on its bedrock slabs, enjoying the trickling creek and looking down the valley you just hiked up. This is also a good turnaround point, since the next 0.5-mile trail segment gains lots of elevation and is heavily wooded.

Continue hiking up a narrow canyon on the rustic trail and then climb an abrupt, steep gully. Watch the trail—it can be easy to lose as it switches back and forth over tree roots and lumpy boulders. Eventually you reach a high saddle at 1.7 miles. The trail goes left here and climbs to a small summit with a big view and the trail's end point at 2 miles. This is a great place to sit down and enjoy breathtaking, expansive views. To the east is the west face of a huge granite buttress called Old Ironsides; farther east are the Pikes Peak Highway, a couple of reservoirs, and the flat top of the Rampart

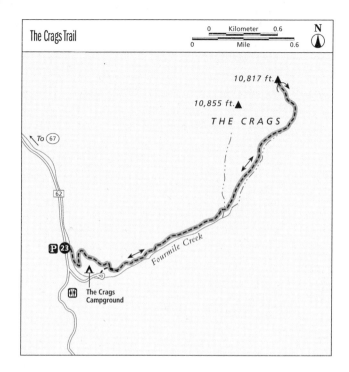

0   Kilometer   0.6

0   Mile   0.6

N

10,817 ft.▲

10,855 ft.▲

THE CRAGS

To (67)

62

P 23

Fourmile Creek

The Crags
Campground

Range. On a clear day you can even see the distant prairie horizon. Also check out the ancient weathered limber pines that inhabit this windswept ridge.

To return, retrace the trail. Take care to remain on the trail as you descend the wooded gully below the saddle.

Miles and Directions

0.0   Start at the trailhead next to the restrooms (GPS: 38.873772, -105.123712).

1.2 The trail passes a cliff to the right (GPS: 38.882348, -105.100095). (*Option:* Turn around here to avoid the trail's steepest section.)

1.7 Reach the saddle.

2.0 The trail ends with summit views (GPS: 38.888446, -105.097948). Retrace your steps.

4.0 Arrive back at the trailhead.

24 Horsethief Park Trail

A steady climb leads to Horsethief Park, a high mountain meadow, and ends at a cascading waterfall on the western slope of Pikes Peak.

Distance: 2.2 miles out and back
Hiking time: 1 to 2 hours
Difficulty: Moderate due to technical terrain; 460-foot elevation gain
Trail surface: Dirt path
Best season: May through Oct; snowy in winter
Other trail users: Mountain bikers and equestrians
Canine compatibility: Leashed dogs permitted

Fees and permits: No fees or permits required
Maps: USGS Pikes Peak and Cripple Creek North
Trail contacts: Pike National Forest, Pikes Peak Ranger District, 601 South Weber St., Colorado Springs, CO 80903; (719) 636-1602; www.fs.usda.gov
Other: Snowshoes required in winter

Finding the trailhead: From I-25 take the Cimarron Street/US 24 exit (exit 141) and head west. Drive up US 24 through Ute Pass and Woodland Park to the town of Divide. Go left in Divide onto CO 67. Drive 9.2 miles south on CO 67, pass a closed-off tunnel on the left, and go around a curve. The gravel parking area and trailhead is on the left at the other end of the old Little Ike Tunnel. GPS: 38.834308, -105.137386

The Hike

Located off CO 67, a frequently traveled route between Divide and the historic mining town of Cripple Creek, the Horsethief Park and Horsethief Falls Trails (FS Trails 704 and

704B) offers the solitude and beauty of the Rocky Mountains without straying far from the beaten path. The single-track dirt trail ends at the crystalline falls, which spills over jumbled granite boulders. The waterfall is most dramatic in early summer, when it's swollen with snowmelt from Sentinel Point, a spur of Pikes Peak. Although steep at the beginning, the trail is perfect for families and kids. It's also a great winter hike on snowshoes.

Most of the elevation is gained during the first 0.5 mile of the hike. Departing from the right corner of the parking lot at 9,740 feet on the east side of the highway, the Horsethief Park Trail climbs briskly above the road and rounds a wide switchback. The path traverses a closed area above an old railroad tunnel and then zigzags back right and enters forested north-facing slopes in a deep valley.

The sound of the highway traffic fades as the wide track steadily ascends, traversing a shelf across a steep slope. Small moss-covered granite boulders scatter about the hillside beneath a dark evergreen forest, offering plenty of shade, and the distant sound of rushing water drifts up from the valley below.

After scrambling over a short rocky section, the trail levels out at 0.6 mile and edges along a rushing creek in lovely Horsethief Park to a trail junction with the Ring the Peak Trail system. Go straight on the main trail, passing placid ponds created by beaver dams, and then head east along the southern edge of a broad meadow. Across the valley, stands of young aspen, gleaming gold in September, cling to hills that rise above the grassy basin. The trail, slowly climbing up Horsethief Park, is a scenic delight. Also look for cabin ruins, perhaps used by the horse thieves for which the park is named.

Sentinel Point, a prominent pointed summit on the west side of Pikes Peak, looms directly overhead. At 0.7 mile the

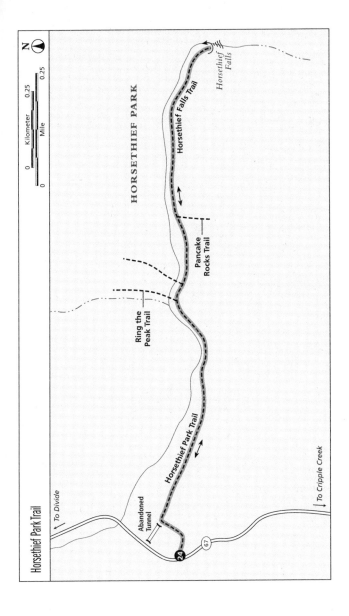

HORSETHIEF PARK

To Divide

Abandoned
Tunnel

Ring the
Peak Trail

Horsethief Park Trail

Horsethief Falls Trail

Pancake
Rocks Trail

Horsethief
Falls

To Cripple Creek

24

67

N

0   Kilometer   0.25

0   Mile   0.25

trail jogs back into the woods at a marked junction with the Pancake Rocks Trail. Go straight on Horsethief Falls Trail and rejoin the willow-lined stream.

After meandering through a forest of tall spruce and fir trees, the trail ends at the base of Horsethief Falls at 1 mile. The cold mountain stream rushes over eroded boulders and cascades down granite bedrock. Cross logs over the stream to rest on creekside boulders on the north side, or climb the mountainside for 0.1 mile to a perch above the falls at 10,200 feet. Either choice is perfect for a quiet picnic lunch or a nap in the sun. In dry years, little water tumbles down the falls.

After exploring Horsethief Falls, return as you came—it's a quick 1.1-mile hike downhill from the falls to your car.

Miles and Directions

0.0 Start at the trailhead on CO 67 (GPS: 38.834308, -105.137386).

0.6 The steep climb ends and the Horsethief Park Trail reaches Horsethief Park. Go straight at the junction with Ring the Peak Trail.

0.7 Go straight at the junction with Pancake Rocks Trail on Horsethief Falls Trail (GPS: 38.833932, -105.123607).

1.0 Arrive at the base of Horsethief Falls (GPS: 38.833898, -105.116203).

1.1 Reach the top of Horsethief Falls. Retrace your path downhill to the trailhead.

2.2 Arrive back at the trailhead.

25 Petrified Forest Loop and Ponderosa Loop Trails

These trails explore Florissant Fossil Beds National Monument's unique fossil record, passing massive petrified tree stumps and old quarries that have yielded some of the world's best fossilized insects, butterflies, and leaves.

Distance: 1.7-mile loop
Hiking time: 30 minutes to 1 hour
Difficulty: Easy; minimal elevation gain
Trail surface: Dirt trail
Best season: Year-round
Other trail users: Hikers only
Canine compatibility: No dogs allowed

Fees and permits: Park entrance fee required
Maps: USGS Lake George; trail map available at monument visitor center
Trail contacts: Florissant Fossil Beds National Monument, PO Box 185, Florissant, CO 80816; (719) 748-3253; www.nps .gov/flfo/

Finding the trailhead: From I-25 and downtown Colorado Springs, take the Cimarron Street/US 24 exit (exit 141) and drive west for 35 miles, passing through Woodland Park and Divide, to the town of Florissant. Turn left (south) onto Teller CR 1 and drive 2 miles to the visitor center road. Turn right (west) and drive 0.2 mile to a parking area at the visitor center. GPS: 38.913545, -105.284834

The Hike

Two excellent and informative hikes—the 0.5-mile Ponderosa Loop Trail and the 1.2-mile Petrified Forest Loop

Trail—explore the unique geological record preserved and protected at Florissant Fossil Beds National Monument, a stone repository of ancient life. The hikes, which are easily combined into a 1.7-mile loop that begins and ends at the monument visitor center, not only offer fun hiking but also are educational. Interpretive signs are scattered along both trails, giving insight into both yesterday's fossil record and today's ecosystems. These easy walks are ideal for family adventures. The Ponderosa Loop Trail is also wheelchair accessible.

Florissant Fossil Beds is simply one of the best and richest fossil locales in the world. Buried beneath the meadows and woodlands is an extensive record of a lost world from thirty-four million years ago. The fossils here are of two types: the minute and the huge. The massive petrified stumps and trunks of towering redwood trees—buried by volcanic mudflows that also dammed the valley and formed Lake Florissant—capture our imagination.

But it is small delicate fossils of tiny insects, animal remains, and fragments of plant life hidden within thin shale layers that make the Florissant Fossil Beds singular. More than 1,500 insect species have been uncovered here, including almost all the fossilized butterflies found in the Western Hemisphere, as well as the only fossil of a tsetse fly, now found in equatorial Africa.

Start your fossil hike at the visitor center. You can pick up a trail map and look at fossils, including small leaf and insect fossils not seen along the trails. Exit out the backdoor to a paved path and a kiosk with safety information. Remember that you're at 8,500 feet above sea level here and may feel the altitude. Bring water, use sunscreen, and keep an eye on the weather in summer. Lightning and heavy thunderstorms are common in the afternoon.

The hike first follows the 0.5-mile Ponderosa Loop Trail clockwise, beginning at some big petrified stumps and exploring the hillside above. The first stump is straight ahead under a canopy. Continue to the next stump pavilion for lots of interesting exhibits and two large redwood stumps, including one with three stumps from a common root system. After climbing stairs out of the stump pit, follow the paved trail 50 feet to a Y junction. Go left on a smooth gravel path. A signpost between trails points the way.

Follow the rock-lined doubletrack trail up and left across a gentle hillside covered with fir, spruce, and pine. At the only trail junction, keep left on the wide trail. The right fork connects to longer loop hikes. The short hike has lots of interpretive signs, some benches, and a couple buried stumps. Return to the large stump shelter and amphitheater, and hike back to the Y junction on its north side. This time go right (north) onto the Petrified Forest Loop Trail.

The trail heads north along the west edge of a broad valley, crossing large meadows studded with glades of ponderosa pine. A trail junction is 100 feet north of the fork. Keep straight on the doubletrack trail. Many interpretive signs are located along the trail, providing lots of information about the fossils, ancient ecosystems, park geology, and monument history.

After 0.3 mile the trail reaches a trail junction just before the aptly named Big Stump. Go left at the junction and hike 0.1 mile to Scudder Pit, a fossil excavation site named for early paleontologist Samuel Scudder. Don't collect any fossils here. Return 0.1 mile back to the main trail and go left to Big Stump. The Scudder Trail is sometimes closed to hikers.

Big Stump, one of the monument's largest fossils, is the remains of a massive redwood tree that was 230 feet high and more than 750 years old when volcanic mud buried its base. In addition to the twelve excavated stumps seen today near the trail, remote sensing has revealed at least forty more stumps that remain buried along the edge of ancient Lake Florissant.

After viewing the colorful stump, head east on the trail, passing a couple stumps, to a hillock dotted with ponderosa pines. The trail turns right here and heads southwest back to the visitor center and parking. More signs detail the area's early history, when competing fossil pits vied for customers who paid to view the stumps or to dig fossils. Near the visitor center, an obscure trail to the Hornbek Homestead cuts sharply left. Keep straight to the trail's end.

Miles and Directions

- **0.0** Start at the trailhead behind the visitor center (GPS: 38.913718, -105.285648).
- **0.1** Reach a Y trail junction north of a stump shelter. Go left on Ponderosa Loop Trail (GPS: 38.913850, -105.286494).
- **0.5** End the Ponderosa Loop at the Y junction north of the stump shelter. Go right to start the Petrified Forest Loop.
- **0.8** Go left at a trail junction to Scudder Pit (GPS: 38.918149, -105.286014).
- **0.9** Reach the Scudder Pit excavation site.
- **1.0** Return to the main trail. Go left to Big Stump.
- **1.7** Finish the hike on the east side of the visitor center.

Options: Florissant Fossil Beds offers six other excellent trails that total almost 14 miles. You can pick up a detailed trail map and get info from a park ranger in the visitor center. All

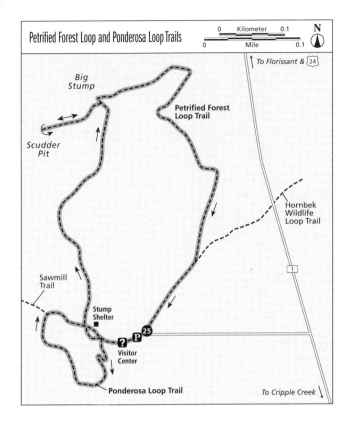

Petrified Forest Loop and Ponderosa Loop Trails

Big Stump

Scudder Pit

Petrified Forest Loop Trail

To Florissant & 24

Hornbek Wildlife Loop Trail

Sawmill Trail

Stump Shelter

Visitor Center

Ponderosa Loop Trail

To Cripple Creek

0   Kilometer   0.1

0   Mile   0.1

N

the trails are well maintained and moderate in difficulty. They have minimal elevation loss and gain, making them ideal for kids or beginning hikers.

Recommended trails are the 4-mile Hornbek Wildlife Loop (keep an eye out for elk); the 3.2-mile Boulder Creek Trail, which ends at a jumble of granite boulders; and the 2.2-mile Twin Rock Trail, with its aspens, meadows, and rock formations.

Appendix: Additional Information

Gear and Guides

Hiking Colorado Springs/Front Range Climbing Company
(hiking guides)
1370 Windmill Ave.
Colorado Springs, CO 80907
(719) 632-5822
www.frontrangeclimbing.com

Mountain Chalet
226 North Tejon St.
Colorado Springs, CO 80903
(719) 633-0732 or (800) 346-7044
www.mtnchalet.com

REI
1376 East Woodmen Rd.
Colorado Springs, CO 80920
(719) 260-1455
www.rei.com/stores/colorado-springs.html

Management Agencies

Bear Creek Nature Center
245 Bear Creek Rd.
Colorado Springs, CO 80906
(719) 520-6387
http://adm.elpasoco.com/CommunityServices/Recand
CulturalSvc/Pages/BearCreekNatureCenter.aspx

Cheyenne Mountain State Park
410 JL Ranch Heights Rd.
Colorado Springs, CO 80926

(719) 576-2016
http://cpw.state.co.us/placestogo/Parks/cheyennemountain

Colorado Springs Parks, Recreation, and Cultural Services
1401 Recreation Way
Colorado Springs, CO 80905-1975
(719) 385-5940
https://coloradosprings.gov/department/76

Douglas County Division of Open Space and Natural
Resources
100 Third St.
Castle Rock, CO 80104
(303) 660-7495
www.douglas.co.us/government/departments/open-space/

El Paso County Park Operations Division
2002 Creek Crossing
Colorado Springs, CO 80905
(719) 520-PLAY (7529)
http://adm.elpasoco.com/CommunityServices/ParkOperations
/Pages/default.aspx

Florissant Fossil Beds National Monument
PO Box 185
Florissant, CO 80816-0185
(719) 748-3253
www.nps.gov/flfo/

Fountain Creek Nature Center
320 Peppergrass Lane
Fountain, CO 80817
(719) 520-6745
http://adm.elpasoco.com/CommunityServices
/RecandCulturalSvc/Pages/FountainCreekNatureCenter.aspx

Manitou Springs Public Services Department
606 Manitou Ave.
Manitou Springs, CO 80829
(719) 685-5481
www.manitouspringsgov.com/government/departments
/planning/post

Mueller State Park
PO Box 39
21045 Hwy. 67 South
Divide, CO 80814
(719) 687-2366
http://cpw.state.co.us/placestogo/Parks/Mueller

Pike National Forest
Pikes Peak Ranger District
601 South Weber St.
Colorado Springs, CO 80903
(719) 636-1602
www.fs.usda.gov